The Old Mermaids Mystery School

Also by Kim Antieau

Old Mermaids Books
The Blue Tail • Church of the Old Mermaids
The First Book of Old Mermaids Tales • The Fish Wife
An Old Mermaid Journal
The Old Mermaids Book of Days and Nights
The Old Mermaids Book of Days and Nights: A Year and a Day Journal
The Old Mermaids Oracle

Other Novels
Broken Moon • Butch • Coyote Cowgirl • Deathmark
The Desert Siren • Her Frozen Wild • The Gaia Websters
Jewelweed Station • The Jigsaw Woman • Killing Beauty
Mercy, Unbound • The Monster's Daughter
Queendom: Feast of the Saints • The Rift
Ruby's Imagine • Swans in Winter
Whackadoodle Times • Whackadoodle Times Two

Other Nonfiction
Answering the Creative Call
Certified: Learning to Repair Myself and the World in the Emerald City
Counting on Wildflowers: An Entanglement
MommaEarth Goddess Runes
The Salmon Mysteries: a Reimagining of the Eleusinian Mysteries
Under the Tucson Moon

The Old Mermaids Mystery School

Kim Antieau

Green Snake
PUBLISHING

The Old Mermaids Mystery School
by Kim Antieau

Copyright © 2020 by Kim Antieau

ISBN: 978-1-949644-51-7

All rights reserved.

No part of this book may be reproduced without written permission of the author.

Cover Painting by Rachel Slick.

Thanks to Nancy Milosevic.

http://www.kimantieau.com
www.kimantieau.smugmug.com
www.patreon.com/kimandmario

Published by Green Snake Publishing.
www.greensnakepublishing.com

To all the Old Mermaids Novices

Contents

Introduction *11*

Mystery One
    Be Here Now *16*
    Tale: Sister Sheila Na Giggles Mermaid and the Rocky Path *23*
    Recipe: Songbird Soup/Tea/Morning Porridge *33*
    Practice *36*

Mystery Two
    Be Full of Yourself *47*
    Recipe: Full Moon Libation *56*
    Menu for the Tea Shell: Summer Sunrise Tea *58*
    Tale: Sister DeeDee Lightful Mermaid Sees the Lightful *59*
    Practice *69*

Mystery Three
    Embrace the Wild *76*
    Tale: Sister Bea Wilder Mermaid Understands *83*

Recipe: Sunshine **86**
  Wisdom: Ability to Respond **91**
  Practice **96**

Mystery Four

  Live Your Siren Song **101**
  Recipe: Singing Up the Sun **110**
  Tale: Sister Lyra Musica Mermaid and the Seeker **112**
  Practice **120**

Mystery Five

  Cultivate Joy **127**
  Tale: Sister Laughs a Lot Mermaid and Jack **130**
  Recipe: Make a Goddess **138**
  Recipe: Old Mermaids Treasure Box **141**
  Practice **144**

Mystery Six

  Be at Home in the World **149**
  Menu for the Tea Shell **154**
  Tale: Sister Ursula Divine Mermaid and Kadar's Shed **155**
  Practice **160**

Mystery Seven

  Encourage Your Creative Process **165**
  Tale: Sister Bridget and the Blessing Time **170**
  Wisdom: Old Mermaid Blessings **174**
  Practice: Make Yourself Into an Old Mermaid **176**
  Practice **177**

Mystery Eight

  Make Magic **182**
  Tale: Sister Ruby Rosarita Mermaid and the Sous Chef **188**

Recipe: The Magic Of Blueberry Omelets *197*
Practice *200*

Mystery Nine
Be Wise *205*
Tale: Sister Sophia Mermaid and Victoria *209*
Practice: Calling in Wisdom *215*

Mystery Ten
Love *222*
Tale: Sister Magdelene Mermaid and the Young Woman *228*
Practice *234*

Mystery Eleven
Flow *241*
Tale: Grand Mother Yemaya Mermaid and the Old Sea *245*
Practice: Visiting Your Old Mermaids Sanctuary *251*

Mystery Twelve
Honor the Ancestors *256*
Tale: Mother Star Stupendous Mermaid and the Night Sky *260*
Practice: Gifted Ceremony *262*
Practice *275*

Mystery Thirteen
Accept Mystery *280*
Tale: Sister Faye Mermaid and the Mysteries *283*
The Many Ways of the Old Mermaids *287*
Practice: A Gifted Ceremony for Someone Else *289*
Practice *291*

About the Author *293*

Introduction
The Old Mermaids Mystery School

Welcome to The Old Mermaids Mystery School.

One winter at a writing retreat in the Sonoran Desert, the Old Mermaids came up out of a nearby wash and began telling me the stories that became my popular novel *Church of the Old Mermaids*.

At least that's how I remember it. I always saw the Old Mermaids as mythic goddess-like beings *and* ordinary women trying to thrive in an environment that was barely survivable. They became more than characters in a novel to me and to others. Each one is iconic and down to Earth. Each one struggles yet stays true to herself and her community.

I have an affinity for the old mystery schools where they examined the ordinary and demonstrated the power, beauty, and sacredness in the so-called trivial. I've always wanted to be a part of a mystery school. One week while staying in a house at the end of a canyon in Abiquiu, NM, where a wild bear was wandering the area and keeping us indoors, The Old Mermaids Mystery School just spilled out of me. I wrote it, I asked people if they would be interested in taking a 13-month course, and it came into being in 2018.

This book is the good-parts version of that original online school. It is now a self-directed course that you can do in 13 months, 13 weeks, or in whatever time you choose, in whatever order you want. You will find no dogma here. This is *your* Mystery School. Enjoy it. Make it your own.

Please read *Church of the Old Mermaids* before you begin the school. It will introduce you to all the Old Ems and make the Mystery School a richer experience for you.

In this book, you will find spaces to journal, record your dreams, draw, and answer questions throughout. Express yourself!

Love and blessed sea,

Kim Antieau

Write about how you are feeling and what your expectations are for TOMMS. Then come back at the end of the Mysteries and remind yourself of what you expected and what actually happened.

_____

_____

_____

_____

_____

_____

_____

_____

_____

_____

_____

_____

_____

_____

_____

_____

_____

Journaling

Dreams

Mystery One
Be Here Now

The great mystery schools taught their initiates, pupils, or novices about the daily mysteries surrounding us. If only we could see, hear, feel, and taste what was in front of us, beside us, all around us, life would be beautiful, profound, and liberating. If we could do this, time would stand still. All would be available to us. That was what they taught.

Is this possible?

For the Old Mermaids it was, and it can be for us, too. The first step and the first mystery is:

Be here now.

Yes, we've all heard this again and again. Be present. Don't pay attention to the past or the future (except to learn from one and make sure you have a plan to pay your bills in the other). How does one be present, and for Pete's sake, why would one want to be present all the time, especially if one's present is miserable?

When I was in my twenties, newly married, and living in Ann Arbor, I read a book about Zen. When one is washing the dishes, the author wrote, one should pay attention to washing the dishes and nothing else. I didn't understand why anyone would want to pay attention to doing the dishes!

I tried it anyway. When I did the dishes, I paid attention to doing the dishes. Time slowed. I became extremely aware. I was so aware of the feeling of the dishcloth and the water on my skin that it was uncomfortable at first. It felt as though something was wrong. This was only because I hadn't really paid attention since I was a child.

I knew right then that being here now meant my life would be more sensual, fuller, and appear to last longer. Of course, I was not able to "be here now" all the time—I doubt anyone can. When I am able to accomplish this, it makes all the difference in the world.

"What's all this time traveling about?" Sister Sheila Na Giggles Mermaid has said to more than one visitor to the Old Mermaids Sanctuary. "Yesterday be gone and tomorrow never comes. Be here now."

> **I didn't understand why anyone would want to pay attention to doing the dishes!**

Sister Sheila Na Giggles Mermaid understood this, as did all the Old Mermaids. She is related to the great Sheela na Gig of Ireland. (There are many spellings of her name.) Icons of Sheela na Gig are often on churches. She's shown as a naked old woman, grinning, holding open her vagina. Patricia Monaghan says her name has been translated as hag, holy lady, and "a vulgar word for female genitalia."

She may have been used to ward off evil, for good luck, for

healing, as a warning of the power of the female. It's difficult to figure out what ancient female symbols meant in their time because they are most often interpreted first through the male lens and then through the lens of the Christian Church. As far as we know, the first archaeologists were men. They would find male icons and call them gods, but they labeled female statues as "fertility figures."

Many scholars now call Sheela na Gig a goddess, probably related to the Cailleach, the dark hag goddess of winter. She may represent sovereignty and a connection to the land. In any case, she certainly appears to represent life (through the vulva) and death (her often skeletal appearance).

Sheela na Gig may be related to Baubo, too, although not much scholarly evidence links them. In any case, Sister Sheila Na Giggles Mermaid is related to both goddesses. Baubo is the Greek goddess of belly laughter. She is often depicted as a vulva on two legs. She is the one who lifted her skirt to the mourning Demeter, causing the goddess to laugh, which lifted her grief over the loss of her daughter. (Coyote is a stand-in for Baubo in my book *The Salmon Mysteries*.) Some scholars link Baubo with Hecate.

All three of these goddesses—Sheela na Gig, Baubo, and Hecate—are goddesses of the people, of the Trivia. These goddesses represent or stand watch over the mysteries of life and death. Sister Sheila Na Giggles Mermaid also understands these "trivial" mysteries. She urges us to "get the starfish outta our eyes," to remove those rose-colored glasses, and see life as it truly is. We can do this sustainably by becoming grounded and staying grounded in the here and now. It is then that we can learn from the past without being stuck in it, and we can plan for the future without fearing it.

We all have times in our lives when it is difficult to be present: when we are in pain, sick, or grieving. It is absolutely natural and healthy to be able to disassociate or "go away" during some of those times. However, we want to be able to consciously make those decisions to "go away," not do so out of habit or rote. The more we practice being here now, the more likely we'll be able to face the truth of the world and our lives and make decisions about how we want to live.

How can you be here now? How do you feel about being still? Do you meditate? How about a walking meditation?

What are your feelings about Sheela na Gig and Baubo? Draw them and see how that feels.

Tale

Sister Sheila Na Giggles Mermaid and the Rocky Path

And then . . . the Old Sea dried up, and the Old Mermaids were tossed ashore onto the New Desert. They shook off seaweed, shook off the last drops of the Old Sea, hid treasures here and there along the banks, and whispered sweet nothings into conch shells that now littered the arroyo and looked like otherwordly creatures waiting for the command to come alive again and share their wisdom, beauty, and treasures.

The Old Mermaids grieved, some of them wailed, and some of them curled up on the sandy bottom of the wash like pill bugs awaiting a new and safer world. But one by one and then together, they eventually left the edge of what had been and what was now. They met their neighbors. They communed with the elements, with the Elementals, with the coyotes, jackrabbits, saguaro, and palo verde. They listened to the whispers of . . . everything.

Eventually they dug their fingers into the earth, added water and straw, and built the Old Mermaids Sanctuary. Where all were welcome. The New Desert had become home.

All the Old Mermaids had their place on the Old Mermaids Sanctuary. Sister Ruby Rosarita Mermaid was especially good at cooking—which was something since they never cooked anything in the Old Sea, except perhaps ideas. Sisters Faye and Bridget Mermaids were particularly skilled at figuring out the right songs to sing, the correct words for the enchantments, and the ingredients needed for this or that malady at this time of the year and phase of the moon. Sister Magdelene Mermaid was good at love. Grand Mother Yemaya Mermaid understood the mysteries, all of the mysteries, better than almost anyone or anything.

Sister Sheila Na Giggles Mermaid's sea chanties were quite colorful, and she could fix almost anything while telling a good joke. Sister Sheila Na Giggles Mermaid was mostly known for her frankness. Her honesty could make a person cringe, but she liked to say, "Get the starfish outta your eyes!" Face reality and move on, she'd say. Things will turn out one way or another.

> Grand Mother Yemaya Mermaid understood the mysteries, all of the mysteries, better than almost anyone or anything.

Sister Sheila Na Giggles Mermaid adjusted to life in the New Desert quicker than any of the Old Mermaids. Naturally, the area folks respected her—and kept her at a distance. Most humans do not care to hear the truth about the world or themselves, at least not as a steady diet.

But then there was Mary Connell. She lived on the other side of the ridge, near where Granita Wash crosses Coyote Arroyo. Over time, the community had become concerned about Mary. The Healer and Sisters Bridget and Faye Mermaids had all visited her several times to treat her injuries. Rocks kept falling down on the path she took from her house to everywhere else. They fell on the path, and they fell on her.

This path, this trail, had been there for as long as anyone could remember. Mary Connell said her parents had walked that path every day of their lives. So had her grandparents. It was part of her heritage. Every year—twice a year—her father and her grandmother before him had cleared the path of rocks that had fallen from above. Some people cleared leaves and roots from their acequia twice a year; the Connells cleared rocks off their path twice a year.

> **Lately the rocks fell more often, and it became a never-ending task to keep the path clear.**

It was not an easy task, but it was a possible task. Until lately. Lately the rocks fell more often, and it became a never-ending task to keep the path clear. Sometimes the rocks fell while Mary Connell was clearing the path. She had been struck several times.

"Will you go speak with her?" Sister Faye Mermaid asked Sister Sheila Na Giggles Mermaid. "We have tried, but she won't listen to us."

Sister Sheila Na Giggles Mermaid couldn't imagine what she could say that everyone else hadn't said, but she walked to Mary Connell's place one beautiful blue sky spring day. A coyote followed her partway, and a roadrunner ran ahead of her.

She arrived at Mary's house mid-morning, but no one was about, so she walked down the path toward the garden, the path that ran midway along a rocky hill. Above was a ridge; below was desert scrub. Sure enough, Mary Connell was bent over a pile of rocks on the path.

"Good morning," Sister Sheila Na Giggles Mermaid said.

Mary Connell stood upright and leaned on her shovel.

"Good morning to ya," Mary said. "I'd invite you for tea, but I need to get this finished up so I can get to the garden before it's too hot."

> She leaned over, dug her shovel into the rock pile, and then lifted rocks into her wheel barrow.

"I can go to the garden with you," Sister Sheila Na Giggles Mermaid said. She looked down the hill a bit and saw an animal trail. "Look, we can go that way, go around the rocks."

"How does that solve anything?" Mary asked. "The rocks will still be here."

"But Mary, they are falling daily now," Sister Sheila Na Giggles Mermaid said. "This is all you're doing these days, isn't it?"

"And what of it?" Mary asked. She leaned over, dug her shovel into the rock pile, and then lifted rocks into her wheel barrow. "You work hard, you get things done. You work harder, you get better at whatever you're doing."

"You are certainly working hard. Are you getting better at moving the rocks?"

Mary shook her head. "No. I don't understand it. My father did this. My grandmother did this. I spend a lot of my time removing these rocks, but they keep coming back. I must be doing something wrong."

"Have you thought about moving the path?" Sister Sheila Na Giggles Mermaid asked. "I see the animals are now walking down further. To get away from the falling rocks, maybe."

"Or maybe they're just lazy," Mary said.

"You think the animals could move these rocks if they wanted to?"

"Maybe." Mary was breathing hard and sweating like nobody's business.

Sister Sheila Na Giggles Mermaid laughed. "Mary Connell, I didn't know you had a sense of humor."

Mary stopped and looked at her. "I wasn't joking. Look, this is my job. This is my heritage. It's something I've wanted to be good at my whole life. If I can't get to the garden, if I can't get to the well, then my life is over, essentially. So I have to keep the path clear."

"Or move the path," Sister Sheila Na Giggles Mermaid said again. She felt like she was talking to a stone.

"My father walked this way," Mary said. "And my grandmother. It is my heritage."

Sister Sheila Na Giggles Mermaid shook her head. "Mary Connell, more rocks are falling. It isn't gonna change for a while. That lightning strike up top last spring burned down two of the trees that were holding a lot of those rocks in place."

"I know," Mary Connell said. "I wonder if I should go talk to the Old Woman and Old Man of the Mountains. Maybe they can make the rocks stay up where they belong."

> I wasn't joking. Look, this is my job. This is my heritage. It's something I've wanted to be good at my whole life.

"They cannot change gravity," Sister Sheila Na Giggles Mermaid said. "I will help you move the path. It won't take much since the animals have already started it. And the rocks stop here on the path or in that ditch. They're not going down to the animal path. See?"

Mary looked where Sister Sheila Na Giggles Mermaid pointed.

"I've been doing this for years," Mary said. "If I quit now, maybe I'm quitting just before I get to that point where I will figure out how to do it."

"You're not quitting," Sister Sheila Na Giggles Mermaid said. "You are changing the way you're doing it. You'd just be stepping off the old path a little. In fact, it would mean that you did figure out a better way to do it."

> **Do you want to spend your life on this path, shoveling rocks that are in your way, or do you want to change the path you're on and avoid the rocks.**

"If I do it differently, doesn't that mean I'm saying my father and grandmother did it wrong?"

Sister Sheila Na Giggles Mermaid tilted her head. She did not understand this. She said, "No, they did it correctly under their circumstances. You have new circumstances. So you can decide: Do you want to spend your life on this path, shoveling rocks that are in your way, or do you want to change the path you're on and avoid the rocks."

"It'll mean I won't be working as hard," Mary said.

"That's a good thing," Sister Sheila Na Giggles Mermaid said.

"Is it?"

Sister Sheila Na Giggles Mermaid nodded. "In this case, it definitely is. And it might save your life. You don't want to get hit by any more rocks."

"Well, there's no guarantee I won't ever get hit by any rocks," Mary Connell said.

"That be true."

Mary Connell dropped her shovel on top of the rocks in the wheel barrow.

"All right," she said. "I'm ready to change this trail. But first, let's eat lunch. I'm so hungry. You'll join me?"

"I never turn down an invitation to lunch. Whatcha got?"

"Stone soup, of course," Mary Connell said.

Sister Sheila Na Giggles Mermaid laughed. "There's that humor again, Mary Connell."

Mary Connell shrugged as they walked away from the rocks, down the path toward her house. "Who says I'm joking?"

What things in your life do you do over and over just from habit? Do you need to change any of these things? If so, how would you change them? Explore these through writing and/or art.

_____
_____
_____
_____
_____
_____
_____
_____

Recipe

Songbird Soup/Tea/Morning Porridge

• First thing in the morning, get an empty glass jar with a lid. Put about an inch of water in the jar.

• Go outside, barefoot if you can.

• Hold the jar in one hand and the lid in the other.

• Listen.

• When you hear the song from a songbird—or any bird—scoop the jar through the air, without spilling the water, and then quickly put the lid on the jar.

• Thank the bird for the song and gently shake the song and the water together.

• Go back in the house.

• If you're making soup, just pour the song water into the pot. If you're making tea, pour the song water into the kettle. If you're making oatmeal or any kind of porridge, use the song water as part of the liquid.

• As always, thank the spirits of the food for this blessing. Afterward, you will find you are singing all day long!

Look at the ordinary things in your life: like buttons, threads, keys, shoes, purses. What magic do they hold? Write about one of these special ordinary things.

Practice

Become aware of your rooted cousins: the trees, bushes, flowers. Stop and become still with them. Become aware of your feet on the ground. Maybe you can feel your socks or your shoes. Perhaps you feel the ground beneath your shoes. (Try this barefoot now and again.) Imagine roots growing from the soles of your feet and traveling down into the ground. The roots go deep. They find other roots and gently intertwine with them. Your roots may go all the way to the center of the Earth where you soak up healing and energy from the core of the planet. You are now grounded and rooted.

Then become aware of what you hear in the distance. Let that go and become aware of what you hear in-between you and the distant sounds. Let that go and become aware of what you hear close to you, maybe even in your own body.

Let sound go, and do the same thing with sight: distant, near-distant, close up. Let that go and try it with smell, although it's a little hard to smell far away. Then do the same with what you feel on your skin: the air, your clothes, your hair.

End with becoming aware of your feet again and gently drawing your roots back up into your body.

You can end this practice here or continue it by focusing on one nearby plant. Stay still and look at it. Listen for it. Close your eyes or keep them open, but see if you learn anything about this plant just by being near it. Take notes afterward if you like, and then research what you learned.

For instance, I once did this exercise with a plant out in a field. I didn't know what it was. The impression I got from it was that it lived as a community and it could help with lung issues. Later I researched it and discovered it was coltsfoot, and it has a rhizome from which many plants grow—a kind of community. Coltsfoot is used for lung problems, particularly asthma and bronchitis.

At the time, I was having respiratory issues. I didn't go out and get coltsfoot to ingest. (For one thing, there is some toxicity related to coltsfoot.) Instead, I hung out with the plant for a while, figuring the reason I had actually seen it—for the first time in a place I often visited—was probably because it had some "medicine" for me.

You don't need to get any "messages" from plants. It is enough that you are still for a bit with them. This exercise will help you Be Here Now.

Write or draw your experiences. Write or draw again and again.

_____

_____

_____

_____

_____

_____

Try to be aware of how much time you spend ruminating about the past or planning for or worrying about the future. You don't have to change anything. Just become aware of your process.

Journaling

Dreams

Drawing

Mystery Two
Be Full of Yourself

Imagine you are admitted to the sacred mystery school of the Delphic Oracle. You take the long journey up the winding mountain roads to Delphi, in Greece. You're thinking that perhaps one day, with training, you will become the Pythia, the Oracle. For now, you stand on the threshold to the sanctuary, looking around at a kind of campus in the wild, where Greek temples, smaller nondescript buildings, and stone and dirt pathways fit perfectly into the landscape as though they had always been there.

You are in awe of your surroundings. Above you is a beautiful blue sky, surrounding you are sacred olive trees and the massive Doric columns of the Temple to Apollo. Then you see the other women, moving in a line toward an almost hidden building amongst the olive trees. One of them motions to you, and you follow. One by one, each woman touches the space above the door with the fingers of her left hand, then takes a step down, and goes into the building. When you get close enough, you see the letters carved into the lintel. It reads "know thyself." It is not what you expected, but you know immediately that this is your first teaching here. You reach up and touch the letters, and then you follow the other initiates into the semi-dark building. You are ready to begin.

Ahhhh.

Now imagine you have traveled down the long winding path of your life so far. The path turns into an arroyo—a dry wash—and you walk in the beach-like sand and wonder where is the ocean? You step out of the wash and discover that you are standing on the threshold between the Old Sea and the New Desert.

You look up and see a sky more blue than any blue you have seen before. The ground is hard and stony. As far as you can see are bushes and cacti, each with thorns that can pierce your skin. You will have to tread carefully here.

A coyote howls in the distance. The sound is plaintive, lonely. Another coyote joins the first and then another. Suddenly, it is a party of howling coyotes. Above you, a crow flies, her wings noisy in the dry air. Far above her, a red-tailed hawk circles. "Do not be afraid," the hawk seems to say.

As you look down again, you notice a path winding through the desert. It is part pink dirt and part pinkish-red flat stone. It is free of rocks, thorns, scorpions, and other hazards. You begin to walk through this strange place, following the red path. Jackrabbits stop to watch you for a moment before going back to their grazing. Birds are everywhere, some quiet, some singing, some brightly-colored, some perfectly camouflaged by the flora.

Eventually you come to a wooden sign hanging from a wooden door. It reads "Welcome to the Old Mermaids Sanctuary." The wooden door is not attached to a fence. It is not attached to anything except to the firm desert floor. You open the door and pass through it.

Before long, women—young and old, big and tall, short and small, dark and light—come out to greet you. These are the Old Mermaids you have heard so much about. Each of them tells you how welcome you are and how they've been expecting you. Even if you are shy or normally overwhelmed by the presence of other people, you are not overwhelmed now. You feel as though this is what you have been waiting for, what you have been searching for.

These are the Old Mermaids you have heard so much about.

As the Old Mermaids continue to talk and tell you about the Sanctuary, you all walk toward a house that appears to be growing up from the ground. Like the rock outcropping you passed by earlier, this house seems to be part of the landscape, as if it had been here all along. But it hasn't been. The Old Mermaids created it themselves from the earth, air, fire, and water when they arrived from the Old Sea. In the space above the door, carved into the adobe, are the words "Be Full of Yourself." Each Old Em reaches up and touches the words just before she ducks into the house through the open door. You do the same before you step in. As your fingers touch the letters, you know you are ready to begin.

The truth of the maxims "Know Thyself" and "Be Full of

Yourself" is that they are two sides of the same coin. We must know ourselves to be full of ourselves; if we know ourselves, then we are full of ourselves.

We are taught almost from birth not to be "full of ourselves." Think about what that means. According to society, we're supposed to take in whatever the culture—our schools, churches, and families—tells us and become that which makes them all comfortable, to become who they believe will be of the most benefit to society or the family. It is the job of these institutions—and our parents, really—to enculturate us. It makes us part of the tribe—it helps make us safer, it helps knit us into a community.

> As your fingers touch the letters, you know you are ready to begin.

At least that was the idea. Maybe it worked at one time. Maybe it works on some level even now. It is a good thing for us to be taught to be kind, help others, and share. But what about those other ideas, like the ones where we're taught that we are supposed to be quiet, calm, submissive, *not* full of ourselves? How are those messages good for us or the world?

According to historical accounts, "know thyself" was carved into the lintel leading into the Temple at Delphi where the Pythia, the oracular priestess, presided and prophesied. We don't know if this was the motto of the Pythia. Perhaps it was one of the proclamations from her, one of those obvious "mysteries." Maybe it was her very first prophecy: "Know thyself . . . and everything else is pretty much French toast and powdered sugar." We don't know for certain.

If we know ourselves, if we're full of ourselves, then life is not only easier, it is much more manageable when life gets stormy. So how do we become full of ourselves?

That, m'dears, can take a lifetime. Or a weekend. It comes and goes. At some points in our lives, we know who we are. And then we don't. And then we do again.

This doesn't mean we don't change things about ourselves we find problematic. It does mean we can figure out more easily what comes from us and what comes from the culture.

Think about this. What if you're shy (or introverted), and you've been told to "get out there and be gregarious?" After hearing this again and again, you may start to feel as though something is wrong with you because you would prefer to stay at the edges. Instead, what if you decided, "I would like to learn how to be heard when I want to say something." In the first example, you're taking in the message from the culture that you're wrong to be introverted. In the second example, you understand your true nature, you don't want to change who you are truly, *and* you decide you want to learn skills to get along in the world more easily.

How do we do it? How do we discover our true selves?

We all have so many messages in our heads, in our bodies, perhaps in our genes, from the culture and our families. To sort through those messages and figure out what is actually truth, what is familial or cultural folklore, and what is propaganda from family or culture is a journey worthy of the greatest heras and heroes in the world!

How do we do it? How do we discover our true selves? One of the things we can do is examine our long-held beliefs and/or prejudices. If you believe there is a right or wrong way to do everything, really look at each of those beliefs of right and wrong. How much stress is each causing you? Must you have the towels folded a particular way and the dishes stacked just so? Or maybe you can't leave the house unless you look a particular way. Or maybe it's that you secretly believe people of a certain ethnicity drive a particular way, or people from this or that culture are dangerous, or only immoral people dress this or that way. Or all rich people are bad; compromise is evil; my religion is the best; no religion is the only way. You get the idea. Look at your knee-jerk reactions and try to figure out where they're coming from. Have you heard people in your family express similar knee-jerk reactions? Are these reactions from your true self? Even if you're not sure what your true self is, start asking this question: Is this what I believe or is this something I picked up from the culture or from my family?

In a way, the Old Mermaids had it easy: The world they knew disappeared, and they had to start all over again. In another way, the Old Mermaids had it so hard: The world they knew disappeared, and they had to start all over again.

Our world is constantly disappearing. It is changing so rapidly, all the time. As Sister Bea Wilder Mermaid says, "Things change. Get over it." She is right, of course. How *do* we get over it? If we carry our true selves with us, if we embody our true selves, then we feel more solid. The truth of the world becomes more apparent, and we know what to do and what not to do. This does not mean everyone will be comfortable with you as you embody your true self, however. In fact, you may experience a lot of pushback from friends and family. This is always a consequence of finding the truth. Not everyone wants to hear it, see it, live with it. But isn't it worth going through life as yourself?

Imagine you are at the Mystery School in Delphi. Describe it. Describe how you feel. Who would you meet?

_____

_____

_____

_____

_____

_____

_____

_____

_____

_____

_____

_____

_____

_____

_____

_____

How can you be more full of your true self? How can you encourage yourself to be full of yourself?

Recipe

Full Moon Libation

On some Full Moon nights, the Old Mermaids asked La Luna to help them make tea for the Tea Shell. Often it was Sister Magdelene Mermaid who would pour water into a jar. She'd add a pinch of a pinch of sea salt. Then she would go outside as the Moon began to rise in the sky.

As she held the jar between her hands, she whispered a chant Sisters Faye and Bridget Mermaids had taught her: "Hear me, salt and water, your loving daughter. May you join with La Luna to heal dis-ease and put all at ease." Then she held the jar up to the sky. "Dear Moon, I ask you to commune with this precious liquid to create Old Seawater to heal all your sons and daughters. Let me go with the flow of the Old Sea. May it be so."

She poured a little of the water onto the ground to honor the New Desert. Then she put the top on the jar and set it where it would be in full view of the Moon and left it all night.

In the morning, one or more of the Old Ems retrieved the jar, poured a bit on the desert floor in thankfulness, and then took it into the Tea Shell and used it to brew tea. Or sometimes they would take a spoonful of it like one would take medicine. The taste of moonbeams first thing in the morning was always a lovely way to begin the day.

Recipe for Full Moon Libation

Ingredients:
One jar with lid.
Water to fill the jar.
Pinch of a pinch of sea salt.
A chant or rhyme or blessing to honor Water, Salt, and Moon.
A Full Moon.

Instructions:
Fill the jar with water. Add salt. Take the jar outside and sing praises to the elements as you ask them to mix together to create a healing brew. Pour an offering onto the ground. Screw on the lid. Put the jar in a safe place where the moon beams will find it. In the morning, the jar and water will be filled with moonlight and healing. Use at your discretion.

Menu for the Tea Shell

Summer Sunrise Tea

- Love Song of the Curved-bill Thrasher Tea
- Wisdom of the Palo Verde Tree Whispered to the Night Tea
- You Are Such a Carrot Soup
- Beans, Beans, We're Mermaid Queens Soup
- No Sand in This Wich (your choice of Grumbling Greens or Toasted Purty Peppers)
- Love Cookies made by Sister Magdelene Mermaid
- Moon Secrets Honey Pie Cookies

Tale

Sister DeeDee Lightful Mermaid Sees the Lightful

When the Old Sea dried up and the Old Mermaids found their way onto the shore of the New Desert, Sister DeeDee Lightful Mermaid did not immediately find her land legs. This was unusual and unexpected because Sister DeeDee Lightful Mermaid was usually the life of any given party. Even those parties that were not given but just sprung up because she was there.

Once she landed at the New Desert, once they climbed up out of the wash and shivered and shook until they had their land legs, Sister DeeDee Lightful Mermaid felt a bit lost. How could she shine her light in a place where the light was shining nearly always?

Sister Lyra Musica Mermaid was afraid, Sisters Faye and Bridget Mermaids immediately began figuring out the songs and enchantments of the New Desert, Mother Star Stupendous Mermaid watched the night skies with renewed interest, Sister Sheila Na Giggles Mermaid got busy, Sister Sophia Mermaid wisely suggested they build a home, and Sister Magdelene Mermaid fell in love with everything.

Sister DeeDee Lightful Mermaid wasn't certain what to do.

She didn't know the land, so she didn't know who she was. She went out with Sisters Faye, Bridget, and Ruby Rosarita Mermaids to learn about the plants. They all seemed excited and buoyed by the experience. Sister DeeDee Lightful Mermaid felt like she was surrounded by thorns.

And the light seemed too harsh for someone who had spent her life in the watery realms. She was not afraid like Sister Lyra Musica Mermaid. She was not even annoyed as Sisters Sheila Na Giggles and Sophia Mermaids sometimes were. She was more irritated than anything else. Even the coyotes howling at night were irritating to her. She definitely no longer felt delightful.

> **They're just different when you're in the New Desert. Different scales, different tails, depending upon the trails.**

She sought the advice of her sister mermaids, of course. They suggested that she be herself and all would be well.

"Who am I without the Old Sea? What is a mermaid without her tails and her treasures?"

Mother Star Stupendous Mermaid put her arm across Sister DeeDee Lightful Mermaid's shoulders and said, "Of course you still have treasures and your mermaid tails. They're just different when you're in the New Desert. Different scales, different tails, depending upon the trails."

Sister DeeDee Lightful Mermaid understood what Mother Star Stupendous Mermaid meant: Her body had adjusted, but her . . . self had not.

Sister Ursula Divine Mermaid told her, "Go see the Old-Woman and Old Man of the Mountains. It was on my trip to visit them when the Bear and Sycamore gave me my true name. I remembered who I was. You will, too."

Sister Bea Wilder Mermaid offered to accompany her. Normally, she would have been delighted at such a possibility. But she decided to go alone. Truth be told: Not much delighted her these days. Even seeing her sister mermaids so altered was distressing, including those she loved most of all.

Sister Ruby Rosarita Mermaid made her food to take along. Sisters Faye and Bridget Mermaids led a land shanty before she left. And then she stepped onto the nearly invisible path that led out of the New Desert and up into the Mountains where the Old Woman and Old Man of the Mountains lived.

"Watch for signs on the way," Grand Mother Yemaya Mermaid said. "There are always signs."

It was a beautiful spring morning as Sister DeeDee Lightful Mermaid left the Old Mermaids Sanctuary. A roadrunner kindly led the way for a time, leaving X-marks-the-spot prints for her. Above, a hawk circled in the blue, blue sky. Behind her, the other Old Mermaids watched her go, she knew, even though she did not look back to see for certain.

She walked determinedly through the desert toward the Mountains, nodding to the Old Saguaros and Old Palo Verdes as she passed, standing in their shade and the shade of the mesquite now and again. She paused by a Creek that was just barely running to eat the vegetables wrapped in tortillas Sister Ruby Rosarita Mermaid had made for her. She drank the water Sister Bea Wilder Mermaid had lovingly poured into a container that

> A roadrunner kindly led the way for a time, leaving X-marks-the-spot prints for her.

The Old Mermaids Mystery School **61**

Valeria Who Loves the Earth had made for the Old Mermaids. And then she continued walking.

Sister DeeDee Lightful Mermaid walked for hours, days, weeks, months, minutes. It seemed the Mountains were not getting any closer. With every step, she felt less delightful than she had before. As darkness appeared to be right around the corner, she began to worry about sleeping in the desert by herself, at night. Of course, Sister Ursula Divine Mermaid had taught her how to start a fire. But what about the scorpions? What about the rattlesnakes? Mountain lions? She did not know their languages, and this world was too dusty for her liking. Truth to tell, she did not like herself here in this world. She wanted to go back to her old world and her old self.

Just then she heard a coyote howling. No, she heard many coyotes howling. A band of coyotes. She heard the sound of a ukulele, too. She wondered who taught the coyotes to play the ukulele. It was suddenly almost dark, too. She didn't like when that happened. She looked around, wondering what she should do next, and then she smelled smoke.

> **She looked around, wondering what she should do next, and then she smelled smoke.**

She peered around a juniper tree and saw a small campfire near an opening to a cave. She began walking toward the fire when she noticed a woman sitting on a stool near it. At least she thought it was a woman. She was gaunt and old, and when Sister DeeDee Lightful Mermaid blinked, she saw a coyote. And then a woman. Then a coyote.

"You must be Old Coyote Woman," Sister DeeDee Lightful Mermaid said as she stepped toward the light.

"And you must be delightful," Old Coyote Woman said. "Although I can't see any evidence of that. Sit." She nodded toward a log not far from her. "The Old Woman and Old Man of the Mountains told me you were coming. They heard it from the cardinals who heard it from the hummingbirds who heard it from someone else. Who can keep track?"

Sister DeeDee Lightful Mermaid sat on the log. "May I offer you a snack?" she asked. "One of my sisters made it. Dried fruit of some kind. I dunno what. I can't seem to keep track of things going on here."

> She had the worst singing voice Sister DeeDee Lightful had ever heard.

"Why are you telling me your troubles?" Old Coyote Woman asked.

"I—I thought that was why you were here?"

"Here?" She shook her head. "No, I was just playing my ukulele, passing the time. Thought you might like to hear a song or two."

"Um, sure."

And so Old Coyote Woman picked up her ukulele from beside her stool—it was shiny blue—and she belted out a few songs as she played the instrument. She had the worst singing voice Sister DeeDee Lightful Mermaid had ever heard. Plus, Sister DeeDee barely understood a word she sang. But other coyotes out in the desert—or wherever she was now—kept joining in, so apparently they liked it.

When it was pitch black out except for the fire, Old Coyote Woman put down her ukulele and said, "I suppose you have been delightful company since you listened to my songs. And the Old Woman and Old Man of the Mountains asked me to point out this cave to you, just in case you were needing a place to stay. No bears inside. No mountain lions or rattlesnakes. No good company either, I suspect. But you'll be safe from everything . . . except yourself."

"All right," Sister DeeDee Lightful Mermaid said. She didn't know what else to do. So she accepted the invitation.

> **She didn't know what else to do. So she accepted the invitation.**

"Keep walking in the dark," Old Coyote Woman said. "You've got to keep walking in the dark for a while. Then you'll see the light. I promise. Just put your hands out to steady yourself."

Sister DeeDee Lightful Mermaid got up to go. She felt a little strange and wondered if the Old Coyote Woman's songs were enchantments. The best ones usually were. Of course, none of her songs had sounded the "best" to Sister DeeDee. In any case, she felt a bit wobbly. She pulled out the rest of her food from her pack and held it out to the Old Woman. The Old Woman shook her head.

"Never give away all of your food," she said. "Especially in the desert. Where on Earth did you come from?"

"The Old Sea."

"That explains it," she said. "Greedy though I may be, and I be, take half of this back. You'll need it in the morning. Now go on. Your delightfulness is wearing me out."

Sister DeeDee Lightful Mermaid was feeling a bit baffled by it all, but she was not irritated. So that was progress.

She said goodbye to Old Coyote Woman who waved her on, and then she stepped into the cave and walked into the dark. She kept one hand out in front of her while the other touched the cave wall. At first she didn't think she could do it. It was too dark. It was too dangerous. What if she fell? What if the cave went on forever and a day? What if, what if, what if?

She breathed deeply—coughed a bit—and kept slowly walking.

"I have to walk in the dark to get to the light, walk in the dark to get to the light." Sounded like some kind of riddle.

Until minutes, hours, days later, the cave curved and opened up. It was suddenly filled with light—moonlight. La Luna was huge and appeared to fill up the opening above the cave. Maybe she wasn't actually seeing the moon. She didn't know. She only knew that the light felt exquisite. After all of that time in the darkness, it almost hurt to look at it.

She glanced around and saw she was surrounded by rocks and water. Water flowed down the cave walls into a still pool at her feet. She looked down and could see her reflection in the pool. When she looked around at the walls, she could see her reflection in the flowing water, too. Wherever she looked, she saw herself.

"Ugh," she said.

Because she saw that she was not who she had been.

She saw legs where tails had been.

She sank down onto the sand. She was so tired.

How would she ever sleep in all of this light?

> La Luna was huge and appeared to fill up the opening above the cave.

She stared at her reflection. And stared. And stared.

After a while, she didn't see herself. Not exactly. Maybe she got lost in thought. Or maybe the walls reflected her thoughts.

The Old Mermaids Mystery School **65**

She didn't know or care. She saw herself brushing Sister Bea Wilder Mermaid's hair. She did this every night. Sister Bea Wilder Mermaid smiled with delight as Sister DeeDee Lightful Mermaid pressed the brush down on her head and hair.

Then she saw herself in the garden with Sisters Faye and Bea Wilder Mermaids. Sister Faye Mermaid was trying to teach them an old sea shanty, and she and Sister Bea Wilder Mermaid kept changing the words until finally Sister Faye Mermaid said, "Be careful. You may mix up the words so much that you change each other into frogs."

She saw herself sitting up late with Grand Mother Yemaya Mermaid, in the near dark, as Grand Mother made quilts for them all. She listened as Grand Mother Yemaya Mermaid wondered out loud what kind of world they had stumbled into. Until finally, as Grand Mother stitched the hum of a hummingbird into the quilt using mermaid's hair as thread, she said, "Oh, but what a place we've come to. I am in wonder all the while."

"Grand Mother," Sister DeeDee Lightful Mermaid said, "you are always in wonder all the while. It is only one of the many reasons we love you so."

Oh, but what a place we've come to.

Sister DeeDee saw herself with all the other Old Mermaids, sitting out by the garden feasting on something Sister Ruby Rosarita Mermaid had cooked up. They were laughing and having a good time. Even when they weren't, they were together.

Sister DeeDee Lightful Mermaid reached out her hand to touch her reflection. Maybe she didn't feel like herself, but she acted like herself. Perhaps that was what was important, for now. When she acted as if . . . there was no "what if?"

She smiled at her reflection. Then she chuckled.

What a strange place this was. In a way, it reminded her of their home in the Old Sea. Only . . . much drier. She laughed. Sometimes things were so simple.

Then she curled up on the familiar sand and fell asleep.

She dreamed of waves . . . waves of love and familiarity.

She opened her eyes in the morning to see the bright blue sky above her. The huge moon was gone. Most of the water was gone, too. Only a small puddle pooled at her feet. She jumped up and hurried out of the cave. It took a much shorter time to get out than it had to get in.

Old Coyote Woman was nowhere to be seen . . . although up on a ridge in the near distance, Sister DeeDee Lightful Mermaid thought she saw a big old coyote humming to some tune.

Sometimes things were so simple.

She looked around and saw she was much closer to the Sanctuary than she had thought. So she hurried through the desert toward home, toward the Old Mermaids. She felt nearly like her Old Self again. Well, that wasn't quite right. She felt like her New Self, and that was just fine with her.

Pretend you are new to your life and world. Look at some of the things you do or own in a completely different light. How could you reinterpret them?

_____

_____

_____

The Old Mermaids Mystery School

Practice

Notice which of your beliefs are from the culture or your family. Ask yourself if these beliefs actually reflect reality. Are they serving you?

_____

_____

_____

_____

_____

_____

_____

_____

_____

_____

_____

_____

Connect with Natural places you enjoy. You choose how.

Journaling

Dreams

Drawing

Mystery Three
Embrace the Wild

Imagine again that you have been admitted to the sacred mystery school of the Delphic Oracle. You say goodbye to your family, for now, and take the long journey up the mountain roads to Delphi. Perhaps one day with training, you will become the Pythia, the esteemed Oracle, able to help your community members make their way in the world.

When you arrive, you stand on the threshold to the sanctuary, looking around at a kind of campus in the wild, where at first you see only trees but eventually, your eyes adjust and you discern buildings amongst the wild, along with stone and dirt pathways fit perfectly into the landscape as though they have always been there. And maybe they have been.

Flowering vines snake up around wooden poles on either side of the open entrance to the area. Between the green of the leaves and the bright colors of the flowers, you observe some kind of writing or markings, but you don't focus on it. In the near distance, you see deer grazing. In another direction, you think you spot some kind of wild cat lounging under the sun.

You feel a rush of excitement as you step between the two pillars and into the sanctuary. Above you, round white clouds dot the sky. Surrounding you are sacred olive trees. Then you see other women, dancing in a circle in an open space next to an almost hidden building amongst the olive trees. One of the women sees you and motions you over.

You walk to the dancing circle. You hear no music. Yet the women dance. They smile as they move their arms and legs and bare feet over the ground.

"What are you dancing to?" you whisper.

The women laugh. One of them takes your hand and draws you into the circle. At first you move awkwardly, but you move. You watch the women and try to follow their movements after you slip off your shoes. The flat stones and sand feel luscious against your bare feet. On one of the flat stones is written these words: "Embrace the Wild." As you mouth those words, you begin dancing in earnest. You feel or sense something. Is it the rhythm of the place? The women? The world? All of it. Your journey has truly begun.

Ahhhh.

Now imagine you have traveled down the long winding path of your life so far. The path turns into an arroyo—a dry wash—and you walk in the sand and wonder where is the beach? Where is the ocean?

You look up and see a sky wider and bluer than any sky you have seen before. The ground is hard and stony. As far as you

> **You feel a rush of excitement as you step between the two pillars and into the sanctuary.**

The Old Mermaids Mystery School

can see are bushes and cacti, each with thorns that can pierce your skin. You will have to tread carefully here.

A group of coyotes howls in the distance. Above you, a crow flies, and you can hear her wings in the dry air. And then a bobcat crosses the wash in front of you. She stops and looks at you, as if to say, "Follow me."

You step out of the wash, and you follow the bobcat. You see a path winding through the New Desert. It is part pink dirt and part pinkish-red flat stone. Eventually the bobcat disappears. You keep walking. You listen to the birds singing, you see jackrabbits grazing, you hear coyotes howling. Despite the strangeness of it all—or maybe because of it—you sense a rhythm, a song, a sound. You can't really describe it in words. But you begin to feel the place. You begin to feel its wild nature connecting with your own.

Eventually you come to a sign in the desert, a wooden sign hanging from a wooden door. It reads "Welcome to the Old Mermaids Sanctuary." The wooden door is not attached to a fence. It is not attached to anything except the ground, except to the firm desert floor. You open the door and pass through it.

> You listen to the birds singing, you see jackrabbits grazing, you hear coyotes howling.

A group of women come toward you. They seem to be dancing. All around them is the New Desert and all the creatures within, it seems. Sister Bea Wilder Mermaid is the first to greet you, and she says, "Welcome to the wild, sister!"

And you know you are in the right place.

Embracing the wild has nothing to do with embracing chaos. It is nearly the exact opposite. Embracing the wild is all about embracing Nature and understanding her rhythms. Once we do that, many things become more manageable. Once we embrace the wild, once we dance to the rhythms of Nature—which are our own rhythms—life feels less chaotic. Even when it is chaotic, we know eventually we will settle into our natural rhythms.

> **Embracing the wild is all about embracing Nature and understanding her rhythms.**

Naturalists, permaculturists, and various kinds of artists spend a lot of time observing our world. For the naturalists, this helps them know when and where they can observe wild creatures and find wild plants. For the permaculturists, it helps them plan their gardens. For photographers, observation helps them know when and where to go to get the best photograph. This is the same for artists using a canvas: They are both looking for the best light and the best views.

It is such a natural thing to do—observe our world—and yet observation gets lost in our everyday rush to do our everyday everything. In this rush, we get out of step. We lose the rhythm of our lives.

Some of us were lucky enough to be raised in environments where we were able to slip into the rhythm of Nature as children. Instead of fighting Nature, we learned to embrace the wild. And now once we begin observing our surroundings, we understand better what is going to happen next. Life begins to make sense.

For instance, someone who lived in our little rental house in Washington before us planted hydrangeas on the south side of the house. Every year this bush bloomed beautifully, and then the sun fried it within days. An observant gardener might have planted the hydrangeas on the north side of the house to avoid this.

We got ants every year in that same house. Sometimes they were the bigger black ants; most of the time they were the smaller black ants. They came in under the door. People who visited our house during this time, especially kids, were often surprised that we didn't spray to get rid of them. I explained, "They come in for two weeks in the spring and then they're gone. I put down peppermint oil, which they don't like. And if they really get excessive, I apologize and vacuum them up." But I didn't poison myself or my house to get rid of a few ants! I understood that the ants were not coming inside forever because I had paid attention to their patterns.

Once we go with our own rhythms rather than trying to force ourselves to be otherwise, life is peachier. Nature is all about cycles, all about rhythms.

Embracing the wild is all about understanding your environment. What seems chaotic often is Nature doing its thing. People got so angry at the deer where we lived in Washington state for eating their flowers. My father used to say he planted enough for himself and the deer. I put up a fence for my veggies, and I tried to plant flowers the deer didn't like. I knew that if I planted something they did like, they were not being evil deer: They were responding to what seemed like an invitation to dinner!

If you know that the east wind brings cold in the winter and heat in the summer and the west wind brings snow in the winter and rain in the spring, then you know you can sometimes predict the future. At least the weather future.

Everywhere in the world it is easy to grow zucchini. Except where I lived in Washington state. For those of us who were close to the river where it was windy most of the time, we had problems with mold brought in on the wind. I railed against this for many years, feeling like a failure because I couldn't grow zucchini to save my life. Then I just stopped trying. One year I had a volunteer squash grow out of my compost pile. It was magnificent. Near the end of the summer it got the mold, but it was grand before that.

Embracing the wild is about understanding our own rhythms, too, and not fighting against them. I think for many of us it was easier to follow our rhythms when we still bled. Once we stopped bleeding, our own rhythms weren't as obvious. That just means we may have to try a little harder to find our own dance.

Once we go with our own rhythms rather than trying to force ourselves to be otherwise, life is peachier.

Nature is all about cycles, all about rhythms.

So go out there and embrace the wild!

How will you embrace the wild?

_____

_____

_____

_____

_____

Tale

Sister Bea Wilder Mermaid Understands

Sister Bea Wilder Mermaid is startled, perplexed, and confused when she and the Old Mermaids land in the New Desert. But she knows they cannot go back. The New Desert is their New Home. She remembers what Grand Mother Yemaya Mermaid always says, "Look to Nature. All answers can be found in that which is naturally wild."

And so once the Old Ems step out of the wash upon their arrival in the New Desert, Sister Bea Wilder Mermaid sets out to find the flow and rhythms of the New Desert . . .

At first, all seems chaotic. It is so different from what she has known. But she stands her ground, she breathes deeply, and she waits.

In a moment, an hour, a day, a year, a thousand years, she sees, hears, feels, tastes the new world. At first, nights and mornings are cool and the days are warmer. The prickly things grow beautifully-colored flowers. Shrubs blossom. Flowers grow up from the hard desert floor: often golden yellow but sometimes red or purple or white. Small owls stand in saguaro cavities making a strange squeaking noise. And other birds are everywhere hatching other birds. Sister Bea Wilder Mermaid is glad to make all of their acquaintances.

Then she begins seeing bobcats and coyotes walking the desert with their children. She introduces herself, but they often do not seem to know or understand her, and they continue on their way.

The days grow hotter. The wind usually arrives from the west when it comes. Flowers disappear. Lizards appear. Snakes with rattles on the end of their tails slither around the New Desert. They move like Old Mermaids did in the Old Sea. Sister Bea Wilder Mermaid nods respectfully each time she encounters one and then steps out of the way.

She soon discovers the dry wash is cooler than the rest of the desert, especially if she finds a spot between mesquite trees. Sometimes she just stands wherever she is and lets the silence throb around her. At night, under a full moon, she watches mice with wings swoop down to the tall people-like cacti.

The days throb with heat, and the nights are little different, except dark. One day the wind shifts. It comes from the south. She feels a strange pressure in the air. Soon it begins to rain. It is as if the entire Old Sea is being dropped on the desert. Flowers bloom again. Javelinas gorge on the fruit of the prickly trees. Baby lizards run everywhere. The prickly trees swell after the rains. Birds and butterflies fill the skies.

> **At night, under a full moon, she watches mice with wings swoop down to the tall people-like cacti.**

And then the wind shifts again. Heat makes the desert throb. When Sister Bea Wilder Mermaid thinks she cannot bear the heat, it begins to cool slightly, and then more dramatically.

Small birds with whirring wings and long bills are everywhere. The world becomes golden in many places.

Life moves faster and cooler. The world feels relaxed and playful. At night sometimes it is so cold it hurts. Jackrabbits graze everywhere, finding goodies on the desert floor.

It begins to warm up. The wildflowers bloom, and the desert is yellow and purple in spots. The birds begin mating and laying eggs again . . .

. . . Sister Bea Wilder Mermaid takes a breath, closes and opens her eyes. She looks behind her where the Old Mermaids wait. She can tell them now if the heat becomes too much to bear, just wait. The rain will come. If the rain fills the washes and threatens to flood the world, she can say, just wait. The heat will come again. And then the cool. And then the flowers. And the babies. And the heat. No chaos here. Just the wild and the wild things.

Recipe

Sunshine

Imagine a woman came out of the dust one afternoon and stepped into the Old Mermaids Sanctuary. She came from far away, maybe through time, maybe through space. She called herself Bisa, and she held out her closed fist when the Old Mermaids came to greet her. She turned her fist slowly and then uncurled her fingers to show them what rested in her palm.

The Old Mermaids gasped.

"What are they?" Sissy Maggie asked. "It looks like a thousand tiny suns."

"When I left my country so far away," Bisa said, "I brought these grains to trade for stories. The grains were yellow, like these grasses I see now and again. When I got to the New Desert where the Sun shines as often as it does at home, I took them out and looked at them, and they were golden. They are yours now." She poured them into Grand Mother Yemaya Mermaid's and Mother Star Stupendous Mermaid's hands.

"Now, can I hear your stories?" she asked.

"Oh, come into our home," Sister Laughs A Lot Mermaid said. "We will feed you after your long journey. We want to hear your stories."

The Old Mermaids created a feast for Bisa while she told stories about her home.

"This grain comes from the Sun," Bisa told the Old Mermaids. "My mother told me that many generations ago, we did not see the Sun for some time. All the shamans and medicine people from all around tried to convince the Sun to come out again, but the Skies were gray. Nothing would grow. And then from far away, we saw someone coming. It seemed it took forever for them to arrive, but arrive they did. It was a woman and her gray cat. She called him Airy. She never told us anything about the cat. He was just there. The villagers said he was really a little boy—some of them saw him running around at night. The woman was a little paler than I am, but she had stars in her eyes.

"She met with the villagers who wanted to know all about her. She wouldn't tell them anything. Except that she could bring back the Sun if they would feed her and her cat for seven days and if they would give them a place to sleep for seven nights.

"Of course the village elders agreed to this. What could it hurt? And so on the first day, food and water was brought to her and her cat. She stayed with one of the village elders. She ate the food. At night she slept. In the morning, she ate the food again. Sometimes she took a walk around the village. Once or twice she went out to the well. She didn't talk to anyone. She was not unfriendly, but she was not social. And the cat tagged along with her always. The story went around that she slept with her eyes open, and you could see the stars moving as the Earth traveled through space in the night.

> **She met with the villagers who wanted to know all about her. She wouldn't tell them anything.**

"A week went by. The Sun was still nowhere to be seen.

"The villagers made the woman a feast for her last night in the village. They even gave Airy a fish they had caught. They sang and danced for the woman. Before she returned to the elder's house that night, she told the villagers, 'Dream of the Sun.'

"In the morning, early, she brought a big pot of water to boil over the elder's fire. Then she poured grains just like these into the pot. She watched the grains cook. She stirred the pot and whispered. Airy, the gray cat, stood next to her for most of the time, and then he wandered away. No one is quite certain what she said, but the story I've heard is that she sang something like, 'Give back what you took as I cook. Sun, Sun, come back now or my cat will eat the Moon and you'll be singing a different tune.'"

> She called to the other cooks in the village and asked them to cook up some fish and find some berries.

The Old Mermaids laughed when they heard this. They could not imagine speaking this way to the Sun.

"Of course it was in a different language than the one I am speaking," Bisa said. "So it had a better rhythm. As she cooked, those millet grains got more and more golden. She called to the other cooks in the village and asked them to cook up fish and find some berries. Someone said they saw the cat sprinkling salt into the millet; others said it was a little boy. In any case, the villagers delighted in eating the millet, fish, and berries. The woman told them that the grains held the power of the Sun. Once they ingested the millet and then pooped it out, the Sun would return."

The Old Mermaids laughed and laughed. Because everyone laughs at poop.

"I was told the woman left town and the Sun returned in a few days," Bisa said. "Everyone's depression lifted, and the crops were planted and grew well. Happy endings all around."

"I think there is more to the story," Grand Mother Yemaya Mermaid said.

"Why do you say that?"

"Because you have constellations all over you!" Mother Star Stupendous Mermaid said. "What was this woman's name?"

> **The story goes that to this day, anyone who eats the sun grain will have sunshine in their lives, one way or another.**

Bisa laughed. "Yes, her name was Bisa. I was named after her. The other story goes that she never left the village. She married my great great very fabulously great grandfather and she was admired and revered for the rest of her life. And the story goes that to this day, anyone who eats the sun grain will have sunshine in their lives, one way or another. Of course, I'm not sure if this is the correct sun grain, but I suspect it is. Wherever I go, the sun does shine."

The Old Mermaids laughed and clapped.

"You came for stories," Sister Sophia Mermaid said, "but you are the storyteller."

Bisa nodded. "I suppose you are right. Shall I show you how to make millet now?"

The Old Mermaids began to add millet to their meal choices. Whenever they ate it, they talked about Bisa, who went on her way after a few days at the Old Mermaids Sanctuary. She began going around the countryside telling stories. She picked up some new stories along the way. Eventually she returned home where she continued to tell stories and cook millet for strangers and family alike.

How to make Sunshine

•1/4 cup of dry millet feeds one person (plenty). Wash it before you begin.

•3/4 cup water per 1/4 if you want it creamy, less if you want it firmer, or boil lots of water, toss in the millet, drain water when millet is done to your liking. Taste it along the way to see how you like it. Leave the lid on if you're precise in your measurements of water; leave it partially on if you're not precise.

•Add a pinch of salt if you like.

•If you're making it like porridge, you can add a bit of vanilla as it cooks. When it's done, add maple syrup, berries, bananas, nuts, whatever you like.

•If you're making it for a side dish (like rice), put it on the plate with salmon and/or vegetables.

•Eat it like you would eat sunshine. It's a very flexible grain. You'll be smiling all day.

Wisdom

Ability to Respond

The Old Mermaids always took care of the Old Mermaids Sanctuary. Once they began to recover from leaving the Old Sea, once they made their home in the New Desert, they began to learn the rhythms and cycles of this place.

They quickly understood the consequences of what they did in the New Desert. The neighbors showed them how to grow gardens and encouraged them to put up a fence or wall to keep the plants safe from desert creatures. The Old Mermaids were happy to share their bounty with their wild neighbors. One morning they came out to the garden and discovered all the new sprouts were gone.

Sister Sheila Na Giggles Mermaid looked at the other Old Mermaids and said, "We're not in the Old Sea any more."

The Old Ems still loved their wild neighbors, and they built a lovely adobe wall around their garden. The flying wild neighbors still partook of the garden, but the rabbits and deer did not.

The Old Ems also helped maintain the acequia, a shared irrigation ditch that had been in the New Desert almost as long as humans had been there. A couple times a year, the Old Mermaids and their neighbors cleaned out the acequia. During the growing season, they took turns closing the gates of the acequia so they could water their gardens and then opening them again to allow the water to continue flowing downstream.

Once a newcomer began throwing garbage into the wash upstream, apparently not understanding the wash was a river part of the year. The Old Mermaids accompanied their neighbors when they went to talk to the Newcomer about the ways of the New Desert. Soon enough, they were all hauling his garbage out of the dry wash and showing him how to re-purpose most of it.

> **They did not make decisions based on panic or a sense of martyrdom.**

The Old Mermaids not only tried to understand the wild things and their environment, they worked to be a part of it and not damage it. The Old Mermaids loved, protected, nourished, and cultivated their place in the world, while also aiding their human and wild neighbors.

They did not make decisions based on panic or a sense of martyrdom. They asked, "What is my ability to respond?" And then they took action. If they felt overwhelmed, they stepped back, communicated with the wild around them, with the clouds, with the ground, with their own feet, their own soles, their own souls, and then responded.

The Old Ems were the embodiment of acting locally. They knew if everyone took care of a piece of land or part of a river, all would be well in the world. So they caretook the Old Mermaids Sanctuary.

We can do the same thing. We can choose a piece of land, however big or small, to caretake. We can pick up garbage there or wherever we walk. Research a wild critter from your area. Do any of them need help? If so, consider donating time or money.

I encourage you first and foremost to learn the rhythms of where you live. What direction does the wind come from that brings rain? Which wind brings heat? What tyme of day is it quiet? Noisy?

Listen to the folklore of a place. See if you can figure out what is true and what is rumor.

For instance, where I lived in Washington state, coyotes and crows were blamed for practically everything. If a cat disappeared, the locals were sure it was a coyote. In Washington state, coyotes can be hunted all year long. In reality, coyotes only kill to eat or feed their pups. Domestic dogs will often kill many animals at once, particularly chickens and sheep. Coyotes are most often blamed for these kinds of kills and then destroyed. If coyotes in an area are killed, the remaining coyotes increase procreation. In other words, they make more coyotes.

> **I encourage you first and foremost to learn the rhythms of where you live.**

Humans can create imbalance because they have not observed their environment fully yet, because they don't understand the consequences of their actions.

For instance, back East where the red fox population is almost zero, the incidents of Lyme disease are extremely high. Researchers are now correlating the demise of the red fox to the uptick in Lyme disease. Red foxes ate mice, shrews, and chipmunks who all carry the ticks that cause Lyme disease. Red foxes disappeared because cougars and wolves were hunted out of existence in that area (or nearly). Eventually coyotes stepped in to fill the void, and they are more dangerous to the red fox.

Humans hunting wolves and cougars a hundred years ago or more essentially paved the way for today's Lyme disease epidemic.

Of course, this is not an argument to become paralyzed into inaction by the fear of consequences. It is an encouragement to educate ourselves and then take informed action.

Question the norms, including your own firmly held beliefs about "good" and "bad" wildlife. Look at different sources with different viewpoints. Then ask yourself: "What is my ability to respond?"

What do you believe that isn't actually true or factual?

_____

_____

_____

_____

_____

_____

_____

_____

Practice

1. Learn about your natural world. Observe Nature, including your own nature.

2. If you haven't yet, go back and do the practices from Mystery One and Two.

3. Connect with wild animals. You choose how, but don't approach them or disturb them in any way.

_____
_____
_____
_____
_____
_____
_____
_____

Journaling

Dreams

Drawing

Mystery Four
Live Your Siren Song

Everyone has a siren song . . . It's whatever you do that you love completely. Something fluid, beautiful, all yours.

—Myla Alvarez, *Church of the Old Mermaids*

Imagine walking down the wash. You're on your way to the Old Mermaids Sanctuary, but you're not quite sure how to get there. Someone told you, "Walk until you come to the arroyo. You'll know which one. It has a song louder than the rest. Or different. Or especially for you. That's what you need to listen for."

You walk until you come to the wash, and you hope it's the right one. You hope it doesn't rain and make the wash a river again. You hope the sound you hear is music especially for you, because as soon as you step onto the sandy bottom of the dry river, the music disappears. But you continue on your way. It's difficult to keep your footing in the sand. And it's hot out. You didn't bring enough food or water. You wonder why on Earth you decided to take this journey. But you keep going. You are determined.

After a while, you hear music. You're certain of it. Only you're not certain where it's coming from. You hear it in the souls of your feet. (Yes.) You want to get closer to the sound, so you step out of the wash and walk toward the music. You feel it all through your body now. You walk across the desert, around the palo verde trees, avoiding the thorns of this and that cacti, your legs and feet relieved to be on solid ground again. Now you hear the sound in your ears. It's singing, although you cannot discern any words. The flora seem to move out of the way, and you see 13 women in the near distance. They are dancing to music from unseen musical instruments, clapping and singing as the sun begins to set.

You hurry toward them. One of the women turns and sees you. She grabs your hand and says, "Good! We could use one more voice."

"One more voice?"

"To sing the Sun a good night, and welcome the Moon to our world."

She releases your hand, and you open your mouth and begin to sing . . .

> **What is it you do that makes you feel as though you are in the flow of your life?**

Most of us have heard the admonition that we are human "beings," not human "doings." For the purposes of this Mystery, we will be looking at our "doings."

What is it that you do that makes you feel most like yourself? What is it you do that makes you feel as though you are in the flow of your life?

It is not about what will make other people feel good. It is not about what you think you should accomplish in your life. It is something you do that makes you feel most like you. It is not necessarily even something you do well. It may be something you have always wanted to do, but you haven't tried it.

Part of being full of yourself is living your siren song. Maybe you already know what it is. Perhaps your siren song was one thing when you were in your twenties, but now you've changed, and your siren song has changed, too. What made you feel like yourself at one age doesn't always make you feel like yourself at another age.

> **Part of being full of yourself is living your siren song.**

Perhaps teaching was your siren song when you were younger. You felt so full of your true self when you were standing in front of a classroom. But nowadays, you feel most like yourself when you are sitting in front of a canvas, brush poised. Art has become your siren song.

Living your siren song goes beyond finding just what feels good to you. Eating a candy bar often feels good, but that's most likely not your siren song. Watching baseball and rooting for your favorite team probably feels great, but would that be your siren song? That's a question only you can answer.

I would encourage you to try different things. I've had many activities in my life that I thought would turn out to be my siren song, but it didn't work out that way. For instance, I went back to school a few years ago to study sustainable food systems and permaculture. Not only did I believe I could make a difference in the world by knowing about these subjects, but I thought working in these areas would be my siren song. It was not. I don't view that experience as a waste of time just because it turned out not to be my siren song. What I learned has practical value in my life, and I came away knowing what I did not want to do. That's a good lesson!

I have also been a teacher, a healing practitioner, and a ceremonialist. Although I was competent—and sometimes more than competent—none of these activities were my siren song. I didn't banish these things from my life. Instead, I incorporated them into other aspects of my life, and then they became part of my siren song. Right now, my siren song is storytelling through creative work. Teaching, healing, ceremony is all incorporated into storytelling, and now I feel most like myself when telling stories, either through my writing, photography, or other methods of creation.

> I came away knowing what I did not want to do. That's a good lesson!

I also understand this can change. And it should. Just writing stories for publication was not my siren song. For a few years, I did not enjoy writing because I hated the publication process. I felt straightjacketed creatively. I considered giving up writing altogether. I always wanted to do more with my photography. So during that time when I was wrestling with my feelings about writing for publication, I started taking photographs full-time. I loved it. I could see the finished creation right away, and I was outside in the wild most days. Now this was something I could do for the rest of my life.

After a while, I missed writing. So I decided to combine my written word stories with my photographs. That was when I birthed The Old Mermaids Mystery School. You are reading and looking at my current siren song. Your siren song may be straightforward or it may be a bit circuitous, like mine was. And it may change over time.

If you have no idea what your siren song might be, become aware of that which brings you joy. Explore activities where you're using your brawn and your brain. Be open to trying something new. Maybe you've always wanted to go out zydeco dancing, but you've been nervous about it. Perhaps now is the time to find out if you like it or not. See where it's happening in your burg. Rope a friend into coming with you or go alone.

You get the idea. Even if something turns out not to be your siren song—and most things won't be—you've learned something new.

Beyond finding that one thing that helps you live in your natural flow, you can use your voice to become full of yourself.

Every culture I've studied uses music, song, and chants as part of ceremony and healing as well as for entertainment. Our Ancestors on every part of the Earth have stood their ground and listened for the songs of the stars, birds, trees, mountains. They sang their songs, they called out to the Spirits of Here and the Spirits of There, and they made their wishes known.

> **Our Ancestors on every part of the Earth have stood their ground and listened for the songs of the stars, birds, trees, mountains.**

The Celts knew that when they heard a particular kind of beautiful music they were about to be visited by the faery folk—and maybe even be taken away to faery land.

The Huichol Indians hear songs in the elements which they

then translate to their own language to become songs of power for their people.

In many cultures, knowing the songs of the Natural world makes a person powerful and useful to their community. They listen to the Natural world, go on vision quests, and listen for songs in their dreams.

We know that most societies—if not all—employ music to connect with each other and the world as well as to create ceremony and healing. Mantras are used for personal and public healing. Indigenous people have songs for every part of their lives: pollen songs, sun songs, healing songs, birthing songs.

Shamans and other medicine people create sound to produce trances and connect with the spirits. Besides drumming and rattling, medicine people use their own voices to make these connections, often creating wordless songs to carry them to the Spirits and help those Spirits recognize them as healers.

Over a hundred years ago, Alexander Carmichael collected ancient Gaelic hymns and incantations into the *Carmina Gadelica*. Inside this huge volume are spells, chants, songs, and prayers of the Ancestors of the Europeans. They are songs to connect with the spirit world and the so-called mundane world.

An enchantment is just a "chant." The word chant means "to sing." Most enchantments are a way to create healing and harmony. This is true for music, too. Pythagoras believed music was a way to "create harmonia, the divine principle that brings order to chaos and discord."

When we use our voices to sing, chant, and enchant, we are attempting to bring order to chaos and discord, ease to disease, wellness to illness. Essentially, we are becoming an inspiration. We aspire to inspire. "Inspire" means to "breathe into." In ancient times, to be inspired meant that the Divine had breathed into us, had gifted us with divine guidance. That is certainly how it feels when we are inspired, even today.

We can use our own voices to heal, relax, and inspire ourselves.

Open your mouth and begin to make a sound, a pleasant sound. Do this without using words. Try this especially if you don't think you are musical. Try this especially if someone has told you you can't sing.

> When we use our voices to sing, chant, and enchant, we are attempting to bring order to chaos and discord, ease to disease, wellness to illness.

If you're worried about disturbing your household, wait until everyone is gone. Or go out to your car. Drive to the country. Do it in your bathroom. You choose.

You can begin by chanting the vowels: aeiou. For "a," chant it as "ahhh." Hold the note, stretch it, make it go up and down. Do it again dramatically. Chant each letter as if you are ecstatic. Do each letter as though you are mad, grieving, celebrating. Wail using your voice. But even if you begin weeping, keep the sound going. This is the music of your soul. Express it. Notice whatever you are feeling has a rhythm. After a while, the feeling disperses, whether it is joy or grief.

Sing along with a song you like on the radio, only don't use the words. Don't hum either. Open you mouth and make sound.

Start singing this wordless way to the world. Sing up the sun and moon. Sing to the plants. Sing to the wind.

Listen for the songs of the sun, moon, plants, wind.

Some of my most profound experiences have come when I'm out in the woods singing to the trees and then listening for their songs. When I'm singing to the trees (or other plants), I feel as though I am participating in an absolutely unselfish act. I'm creating a bond between myself and the trees. At least, that is how I perceive it.

In any case, let your voice go. If you are a trained singer, try to be unhindered by that training. This isn't a performance. This is letting your soul, your heart, your being let loose!

May it all inspire you.

Sing. How was the experience?

Recipe

Singing Up the Sun

Now and again, the Old Mermaids went out into the desert and sang up the Sun. Other members of the community came with them. Some brought rattles, all brought their voices. They stood in the gray of dawn facing East. When the Sun was just about at the horizon, they began to sing and rattle and encourage the Sun to rise.

"Rise, Sun, rise! Watch our fun! Watch us run! Rise, Sun, rise!" They did this until the Sun rose. Then they clapped, and sang, "Now we are done!"

The Old Mermaids believed that people somewhere on the planet needed to encourage the great lifemaker—the Sun—to rise every dawn. On some days, they wanted to be those people.

You can do it, too. Standing your ground on the land as night seeps away and the day begins can be amazingly profound, healing, and informative. During those times, you are at a threshold between darkness and light, night and day, sleep and awakening, endings and beginnings. Dawn is a time of enlightening, literally. You don't need to sing or rattle or dance. You can always just wish the Sun well.

Recipe for Singing up the Sun

• Go out before dawn, bringing your voice or a rattle or drum.

• If you like, bring an additional offering of water, a blossom, or a pinch of sage.

• Look to the east and make beautiful noise as the Sun comes up.

• Thank the Spirits of Here and the Spirits of There, thank the Sun, the Sky, the birds, clouds, trees, bees, and ye as you leave and continue your day.

Tale

Sister Lyra Musica Mermaid and the Seeker

As you know, Sister Lyra Musica Mermaid had a bit of trouble when the Old Mermaids first washed up onto the shores of the New Desert. The New World was a little bit too new for her. She worked to understand the rhythms and ways of the desert, just as all the Old Ems did. But Sister Lyra Musica Mermaid was accustomed to harmony, and life in the New Desert was not always harmonious. She often felt uneasy, and this uneasiness made her uncomfortable. Sometimes she wandered the desert looking for something to ease the discomfort.

She walked the desert and listened to the trees. She listened to the thorny ones. She listened to the bushy ones. She heard their songs; she sensed their voices. She discovered when they dropped their leaves and when they grew their fruit. She knew which ones were full of water and which ones were not. Even during the hottest times of the year, she felt the harmony of the place.

She watched for and listened to the animals. She knew she could follow the fox and bobcat into myth. Coyotes brought her music, but she needed to keep her distance. Mountain Lion would follow her to and fro with harm to none, unless she decided she was hungry. The Rattler had stories to tell, but death could await at the end of such tales if Sister Lyra Musica Mermaid was not full of care. No one could part the veils between here and there the way Jackrabbit could.

Still, even knowing all this, Sister Lyra Musica Mermaid felt a bit out of place and out of balance now and again.

One day while she was wandering, Sister Lyra Musica Mermaid saw another woman coming toward her. Her gait was erratic, and she held her hands up to her head. Sister Lyra Musica Mermaid stopped and called, "Are you well? Do you need assistance?"

The woman seemed to see her for the first time, even though she had been heading straight for her. Soon they were feet apart from one another.

"Are you lost?" Sister Lyra Musica Mermaid asked.

"I am indeed," the woman said. "My name is Dolores, and I've come to find my way. I have long heard of the Old Mermaids Sanctuary."

Sister Lyra Musica Mermaid smiled and said, "You are welcome, of course. I will take you to my sister mermaids."

They began to walk through the desert together.

No one could part the veils between here and there the way Jackrabbit could.

"I have been searching my whole life to find a place where I belong," Dolores said. "I feel so lost most of the time."

"I hear you, sister," Sister Lyra Musica Mermaid said. "When we first arrived here, I was—"

The Old Mermaids Mystery School

"I bet you know everything about here," Dolores said. "And you can tell me. I want to be just like you."

Sister Lyra Musica Mermaid was startled. How could this woman decide she wanted to be just like her when she knew nothing about her?

"I can tell this is the place," Dolores said. "I know it. As soon as I saw you, I knew you were the answer. Look at you. You are so at home here."

"Well, when we first—"

"I bet if I had grown up in a place like this, I would know my way."

Dolores began telling Sister Lyra Musica Mermaid the story of her life. She had grown up in a place not like the New Desert and raised by parents who did not understand that she was a seeker who had no time for the trivia of their lives. Finally one day she left and was free of their influence. Dolores told her tale quickly—except when it came to some part of her life where someone had mistreated her. Then she slowed and told those stories with relish. Sister Lyra Musica Mermaid tried to take it all in, but truth to tell, she was relieved when they finally arrived at the "Welcome to the Old Mermaids Sanctuary" sign.

Sister Lyra Musica Mermaid opened the gate for Dolores and then led the way to the garden where Sisters Faye and Laughs a Lot Mermaids were working. The Old Ems rose from the dirt as Sister Lyra Musica Mermaid approached with Dolores.

> **How could this woman decide she wanted to be just like her when she knew nothing about her?**

"This is Dolores, and she has come to visit," Sister Lyra Musica Mermaid said.

"Welcome!" Sister Laughs a Lot Mermaid said. "We love having visitors."

"No, I am not a visitor," Dolores said. "I want to live here. I know this is my place. Oh, look at that dirt! And you planted all of this, and it's growing. That is profound." She took a deep breath. "Yes, I knew it. That is what I want to be. This is what I want to do. Please show me the way to be a great gardener."

> It was her Better Than Average Chili.

Sister Faye Mermaid cocked her head slightly and glanced at Sister Lyra Musica Mermaid who pressed her lips together and shrugged. Soon enough Dolores was down in the dirt with them.

Sister Lyra Musica Mermaid did not see Dolores again that day until dinner when all the Old Mermaids gathered round to partake in some of Sister Ruby Rosarita Mermaid's chili. It wasn't quite the famous chili that had more than once fed everyone on the Old Mermaids Sanctuary and beyond. It was her Better Than Average Chili which was made not only with Old Mermaids' tears but also with seaweed the good neighbors The Pepperman and The Pepperwoman had given them.

Dolores took one bite of the chili and said, "Oh my! This is the best chili I've ever had! I've had a revelation! An epiphany! I must become a chef! That is how I'll make my way in the world. Please, Sister Ruby Rosarita Mermaid, will you train me?"

Sister Ruby Rosarita Mermaid said, "Darlin', I am no chef. I can certainly teach you how to cook."

The Old Mermaids Mystery School

"Oh, what a gift!" Dolores said. "I knew I belonged here."

And so it went over the next few days. Everywhere Dolores went, she was certain it was her place. She was certain she had found her life's work.

When they visited Annie Who Loves Birds, Dolores promised that birds would be her focus from now until the end of her time.

> **Everywhere Dolores went, she was certain it was her place. She was certain she had found her life's work.**

When Dolores went to the Tea Shell, she swore she would now dedicate her life to serving others tea and whatever else the Tea Shell served.

As a rule, the Old Ems were accepting of others. They didn't judge whether someone talked too much or too little. They didn't judge a person by the clothes she wore or the work she did. However, Sister Lyra Musica Mermaid was confused by Dolores. In fact, she admitted to herself that she did not like her.

Since Dolores had arrived, Sister Lyra Musica Mermaid had felt out of balance. She felt like the whole of the Old Mermaids Sanctuary was out of balance. She had brought Dolores into their lives, so it was up to her to remedy the situation. She asked for advice from Grand Mother Yemaya Mermaid who was standing next to a saguaro listening to a thrasher sing.

"It's Dolores," Sister Lyra Musica Mermaid said. "That is why nothing is harmonious any more. She has put everything out of balance."

Grand Mother Yemaya Mermaid looked around and then said, "What is out of balance? The sun still rises and falls. The moon still rises and falls. The thrasher still sings. The air is clear. The water is clear. I see clarity and balance all around."

Sister Lyra Musica Mermaid started to say, "But—" and then she stopped and took a deep breath. She looked around, too. Grand Mother Yemaya Mermaid was right.

"She has only knocked me out of balance then," Sister Lyra Musica Mermaid said.

"Has she?" Grand Mother Yemaya Mermaid asked. "Are you out of balance?"

"I certainly feel off-balance," Sister Lyra Musica Mermaid said.

But why?

"She seems so desperate," Sister Lyra Musica Mermaid said, "and uncomfortable."

"What has that to do with you?" Grand Mother Yemaya Mermaid asked. "You aren't required to be with her."

"But I understand her," Sister Lyra Musica Mermaid said, "in a way. I understand her discomfort. I want her to be at ease."

"So that you will also be at ease?"

Sister Lyra Musica Mermaid hesitated, and then she said, "Yes, you're right."

> She had been seeking answers from all kinds of places.

It wasn't about Dolores. It was about her own unease in the world. She still did not feel as though she belonged. She had been seeking answers from all kinds of places, too, just as Dolores had.

Sister Lyra Musica Mermaid went and sat on the sandy bottom of the wash for a time. Her toes dug into the earth. She breathed. She listened to the world around her buzz slightly. She realized that it all looked and sounded and felt familiar. She supposed that was one definition of home: familiarity. She smiled. That was a step in the right direction.

Sister Lyra Musica Mermaid was late heading out to Flat Rock Woman where the Old Mermaids would sing up the Moon, so she ended up going alone. Partway there, she heard a woman crying. She hurried toward the sound and found Dolores standing near an old palo verde tree, crying.

She looked up when Sister Lyra Musica Mermaid neared. "There's nothing to lean against here!" she said. "No tree that won't prick me to death. No people, to speak of!"

"It is indeed a thorny place," Sister Lyra Musica Mermaid said. "May I help you with something?"

"I keep trying things," she said, "but I still don't feel as though I have a place in the world. Can you tell me what to do?"

Sister Lyra Musica Mermaid said, "No, I can't tell you what to do. It seems like you see someone and then you try to do what they are doing and be who they are being. Why not be yourself?"

Dolores began sobbing. "There is no myself. I'm empty."

"Congratulations!" Sister Lyra Musica Mermaid said. "Sister Sophia Mermaid has said some humans spend their entire lives trying to be empty!"

Dolores chuckled. She wiped her eyes. "I think it's a different kind of empty."

"You just need to find your own voice," Sister Lyra Musica Mermaid said. "Sometimes we need to be still and quiet, and sometimes we can find our own voice with others."

> **She supposed that was one definition of home: familiarity.**

Sister Lyra Musica Mermaid took Dolores's hand. "Come on! We'll sing the moon up."

Sister Lyra Musica Mermaid and Dolores got to Flat Rock Woman just before the Moon rose up over the mountains. The Old Mermaids and Dolores stood on the rock, barefoot. This night, they all chanted, "Ahhhhhhh!" and then "Ohhhhh!" and then they each chose their own wordless sound. Some of them danced and clapped, too. Sister Lyra Musica Mermaid felt as though everything was in balance once again as the Moon rose above the Mountains, encouraged by the voices of the women.

When they were finished chanting and then chatting, after the Moon came up and the women had been silent for a while, Sister Lyra Musica Mermaid said to Dolores. "How are you feeling now?"

Dolores smiled and said, "Full enough."

Sister Lyra Musica Mermaid nodded. "Me, too."

> **Sister Lyra Musica Mermaid felt as though everything was in balance once again as the Moon rose above the Mountains, encouraged by the voices of the women.**

Practice

Find your Siren Song. If you're not sure what your Siren Song is, look around. What is it you do that makes you feel most like your true self? Explore new activities. Remember, this isn't about quitting your job and running off to live at the beach (although that could happen). It's about finding your flow. You can keep your job and still have your Siren Song. In fact, for some people, their job is their Siren Song.

_____

_____

_____

_____

_____

_____

_____

Be still and silent and see what you can "hear" from the Natural world. Do it with intent. Choose a tree, bush, or flower and ask permission to communicate. See if they want to hear a wordless song from you.

For instance, one day I was walking up a hill alone, and I had an asthma attack. I felt very vulnerable. I was a couple of blocks from home, and it was all uphill. I stopped. I thought, "I'm so alone. There's no one to help me. What will I do? Will I die on this hill?" Just then, I felt something. I can't explain what it was exactly. I looked to my left, to the ditch next to me. Several plants were growing up out of the ditch. I can't even remember exactly which plants they were now, but what I felt was, "We're here. You can always connect with us. We're always right here." I felt such relief in those moments and such a connection with the world. I stood with the plants until my breathing evened out. Then I thanked them, and I continued home.

Pay attention to your dreams. Are they telling you something regarding the Old Mermaids?

Journaling

Dreams

Drawing

Mystery Five
Cultivate Joy

Imagine you have been at the Sanctuary in Delphi for a while now. You have learned about yourself and the natural world. You have danced with the other women—maybe you even danced with the Nature sprites who inhabit the mountain and the forest. You have been serious-minded about your studies. One day after a midday meal, you fall asleep on a slab of rock in the sun amongst the olive trees.

When you awaken, it momentarily looks like it is snowing, but then you realize a breeze has come across the mountains and is shaking off the flower petals from all the nearby fruit trees. You get up and begin to follow the rocky petal-strewn path through the olive trees. The air smells of rosemary and sage. You hear the sound of women nearby, and you sleepily follow their voices until you come to a clearing. There, you find your Delphian sisters lounging on the ground and nearby stones while one woman stands before them telling a tale.

You stop and listen. You can't quite hear the words because you're still too distant and the breeze blows the sound away. And then the storytelling woman lifts her garment to show her nakedness underneath. All the women roar with laughter and clap as your Delphic sister drops the cloth back down again and bows slightly. It feels as though the entire mountain shakes in delight as the sisters laugh. You smile and begin laughing as you run toward them. How could you have forgotten how wonderful it is to feel joy?

And so it is at the Old Mermaids Sanctuary. The Old Mermaids are perhaps the most joyful beings in the world. They aren't fake joyful. They don't pretend all is well when it definitely is not. But underneath it all, they rejoice in living, and they are full of joy for their lives with one another.

Joy is often lost in our everyday lives, especially when we struggle with health, money, relationships. Joy often becomes something we need to cultivate. The word cultivate means "to prepare for crops." If we aren't feeling joy spontaneously, it means we need to prepare ourselves for the crop of joy. We need to plant the seeds of joy. Again, it isn't about pretending all is well. It is necessary in life to face reality so that we can work the problems. Yet too often we get attached to stories of failure, sickness, deprivation. When we keep telling these stories, we are strengthening the neural pathways in our brains about sickness, deprivation, and failure.

> **How could you have forgotten how wonderful it is to feel joy?**

We can cultivate joy by catching ourselves when we engage in catastrophic thinking. When we say things like, "I never succeed," "I'm always sick," "I never have enough money," we are cultivating ideas that don't nourish us. If you hear yourself saying, "I never succeed," change your monologue. Tell yourself it's not true and give yourself examples. "I succeeded in getting out of bed today." "I succeeded in making myself breakfast." You can make it into a funny game. "Oh, yeah? You think I'm not successful? I can boil water better than anyone I know."

Baubo lifts her dress and exposes her vulva to Demeter.

Remember when Demeter mourned the loss of her daughter Kore/Persephone? She was so bereft that nothing would grow in the world. All the plants died. No one could do anything to assuage Demeter's grief. One day Baubo comes to draw water at the well near Demeter. (Baubo's name means "belly," and she is the goddess of belly laughter and is probably an ancient goddess and a form of Hecate.) She sees how sad Demeter is, and she offers her condolences, just as so many others have. This means nothing to Demeter. So Baubo lifts her dress and exposes her vulva to Demeter. Demeter smiles, and then she laughs and laughs. The spell of grief and depression is broken. The hills are soon covered with flowers again, and Persephone is restored.

Laughter really is the best medicine.

Cultivate joy in whatever way you can. Be spontaneous. Force yourself to laugh. Make yourself smile. Yes, in this case, I am suggesting you force yourself to laugh and smile now and again if you can't do it naturally. Watch funny movies and TV shows. Life is not meant to be a grind. Do things just for the fun of it. I know you can do it. It will help you bloom.

Tale

Sister Laughs a Lot Mermaid and Jack

Sister Laughs a Lot Mermaid is a lot of fun. She has her ups and downs just like any being, but she does love to laugh. She finds joy wherever she goes, which has led her on an adventure or more.

For instance, one day she was walking through the desert on her way to visit The Pepperwoman and Pepperman when she heard the tinkling of a tiny bell. She stopped and listened. She knew from her time in the Old Sea that the sound of a tiny bell like this could mean the Good Folk were about. Of course, to some, she and the Old Mermaids were part of the Good Folk—and maybe everything and everyone on the Old Mermaids Sanctuary were part of that Other World. She didn't know. She didn't think about it. That would be too close to contemplating existence itself, and that was not Sister Laughs A Lot Mermaid's way. Instead, she walked toward the sound. As she walked, the sound stopped.

But soon enough she was at the lip of the wash. Across the way, she saw what appeared to be a human-sized jackrabbit, standing with its arms crossed, leaning against a saguaro. Sister

Laughs A Lot Mermaid blinked and looked again. This time she saw a woman who appeared at first to be naked or covered in a light brown fur. When she blinked again, she saw the woman was wearing something that was very light brown—and her hair was all white. She had the biggest ears of almost anything Sister Laughs A Lot Mermaid had ever seen before, except, of course, for jackrabbits.

The woman moved away from the saguaro—Sister Laughs A Lot Mermaid wondered how on Earth she could lean against a saguaro!—and motioned to the Old Mermaid.

Sister Laughs A Lot Mermaid crossed the wash and walked toward the woman.

"Hello," Sister Laughs A Lot Mermaid said. "Welcome!"

"Welcome? What do you mean 'welcome' as if this place is not already my home. Who are you to welcome me to my home?"

"I'm sorry!" Sister Laughs A Lot Mermaid said, startled. "I don't recognize you. I'm Sister Laughs A Lot Mermaid. I live with the other Old Mermaids in the Sanctuary."

"Hmph."

"I heard a bell tinkling so I came your way," Sister Laughs A Lot Mermaid said.

The woman uncrossed her arms and seemed to relax. "Ahhh! Then you are exactly who I need. I am Jack." The woman put out her left hand palm up, the way magical beings all over the world greet each other. Sister Laughs A Lot Mermaid placed her left hand over Jack's hand. They held hands for an instant and then

> The woman put out her left hand palm up, the way magical beings all over the world greet each other.

The Old Mermaids Mystery School

turned their hands to shake like other people, only they were shaking with their left instead of their right.

"If you heard the bell, then perhaps you can lead me to it," Jack said. "I got separated from my drove. We had a bit of spat, I got angry, and I walked off, and I forgot who I am."

"Jackrabbits get angry?"

"Who said anything about jackrabbits? Can you help me or not?" She was cranky again.

"I don't hear the bell any more," Sister Laughs A Lot Mermaid said, "but I'll do whatever I can to help you. Where did you last see your bell?"

"If I knew that, I wouldn't need you," Jack said.

Sister Laughs A Lot Mermaid laughed.

"That was not meant to be funny," Jack said.

"Nevertheless," Sister Laughs A Lot Mermaid said.

"I think I was in the dry river," Jack said, "although I can't be sure."

"What's it look like?" Sister Laughs A Lot Mermaid said.

"You ask a lot of questions."

"Are two questions a lot?" Sister Laughs A Lot Mermaid asked.

Jack made a face. "It's small, silver, with a turquoise stone at the center of one side."

> **She listened again and heard nothing.**

Sister Laughs A Lot Mermaid nodded. She listened again and heard nothing.

"I'm on my way to The Pepper's place," Sister Laughs A Lot Mermaid said. "They are great treasure hunters. They used to be bad neighbors when they first got here, but now it's as if they were always here. They're right over the rise."

Jack looked around. "I don't want to forget where I was."

"We could put a big X on the ground to mark the spot," Sister Laughs A Lot Mermaid suggested.

Jack made a noise. "What? You think I'm a damn roadrunner?" She pulled up what she was wearing and pulled down something else she was wearing, and she promptly peed near the saguaro. "There," she said.

Sister Laughs A Lot Mermaid made an X with her heel, too.

And then Sister Laughs A Lot Mermaid led them over the rise and to The Pepper's place. The couple sat out front in the shade, fanning themselves, glasses of tea next to them.

> You've lost your joy. Your *raisin d'etre*. Your heart. Your compassion. We've heard that can happen.

"Welcome," The Pepperwoman said. "Sister Laughs A Lot Mermaid, you have brought a new friend."

"I am no friend," Jack said, "and I'm not new. Far from it. I remember this place before you or this building were here."

"Would you like some soup or tea?" The Pepperman asked.

"She's lost her bell," Sister Laughs A Lot Mermaid said.

The couple nodded. "We understand. You've lost your joy. Your *raisin d'etre*. Your heart. Your compassion. We've heard that can happen."

The Pepperwoman and Pepperman often surprised Sister Laughs A Lot Mermaid. They knew a lot more than one would think upon first meeting them.

Jack said, "Yes! I feel I am quite not myself, although I don't really remember. Have you heard bells this morning?"

"We have not," The Pepperwoman said, "but we will help you find it. Have some tea first, and we'll round up the others."

Jack accepted the tea, and The Pepperman went out and got neighbors from far and wide. Soon they were all wandering the desert looking and listening for a tiny bell.

"This reminds me of the time I lost my marbles," The Pepperman said. "It took us forever and a day to find them and The Pepperwoman says I'm still missing a few."

> They dodged rattlesnakes and thorns and each other's nerves.

Everyone laughed. Except Jack. She looked at Sister Laughs A Lot Mermaid and asked, "Why is that funny?"

"It means he went crazy," Sister Laughs A Lot Mermaid said.

"That's not funny," Jack said.

"Nevertheless . . ."

"I feel crazy right now, and it's not funny!"

"He probably didn't really go crazy," Sister Laughs A Lot Mermaid said. "He was just joking."

They dodged rattlesnakes and thorns and each other's nerves. The sky was brilliant blue. The Old Ems joined the search, of course.

Sister Bridget Mermaid said to Sister Laughs A Lot Mermaid, "This sounds like someone else's magic. It's not always wise to interfere in such things."

"But she asked for help," Sister Laughs A Lot Mermaid said. "I couldn't say no."

"Of course not," Sister Bridget Mermaid said. "We'll just be on the lookout."

"To be sure."

And for a while longer, they wandered. One by one, they told a story or a joke. There was the one about the rattlesnake who lost her rattle but eventually found it where she'd last seen it (at the end of her tail), and she ended up joining a percussion band. Then the one where Old Coyote Woman decided to teach her grandpups about cooking, only everything kept coming out raw. And the Crow who fell in love with his reflection in a pool.

Jack did not laugh at any of it, although she smiled now and again as the day wore on.

"I miss everything," Jack said. "Especially all those jackasses who made me mad."

Sister Laughs A Lot Mermaid laughed.

"I wasn't joking."

"But you said JACKasses," Sister Laughs A Lot Mermaid said.

"It's not funny."

"Nevertheless . . ."

Eventually, neighbors began to fall away as they went back to their respective homes to nap or eat. The Old Mermaids invited Jack to come back to the Sanctuary for a meal.

> **The Old Mermaids invited Jack to come back to the Sanctuary for a meal.**

Jack said, "I am so amazed and appreciative that you all came out to help me. Thank you."

Jack continued to walk back toward where Sister Laughs A Lot Mermaid had first seen her. Suddenly Sister Laughs A Lot Mermaid heard the tinkling bell again.

"Did you hear that?" Sister Laughs A Lot Mermaid asked.

Jack said, "No."

Sister Laughs A Lot Mermaid looked down. They were standing right on the X marks the spot she had created with her heel earlier in the day. She looked across the way and saw eight huge jackrabbits. They were all standing on their hind legs with their arms in the air. Sister Laughs A Lot Mermaid pointed. Jack followed her gaze and saw the jackrabbits.

She began to laugh. "Look at them! Grown jackrabbits acting like humans. How silly!" She laughed and laughed. Sister Laughs A Lot Mermaid laughed right along with her. The desert was filled with laughter.

Then she heard the bell again. She turned and looked at the mesquite tree next to her. There she saw a tiny silver bell hanging by a thread on one of the slender branches. She reached for it and took it from the tree.

> Jack pressed the tiny bell against her chest and then at her throat and finally on her forehead.

"Look what I found," Sister Laughs A Lot Mermaid said. She handed the bell to Jack. The other eight jackrabbits were on their haunches now and no longer looked as big as a human person.

Jack held the bell between her forefinger and thumb and shook it slightly. The sound was pure joy. Jack pressed the tiny bell against her chest and then at her throat and finally on her forehead.

Then she held it out to Sister Laughs A Lot Mermaid. "Here. It's yours now. It's part of me. It always has been. I should've remembered that. It will bring you joy, always."

Sister Laughs A Lot Mermaid took the bell. Jack held out her left hand again, palm up, the way magical beings greet one another. Sister Laughs A Lot Mermaid placed her left hand over Jack's, held it for a moment, and they shook hands.

Then Jack was gone. She ran toward the jackrabbits, into dusk. Soon enough Sister Laughs A Lot Mermaid could no longer see her, could barely see the nine jackrabbits hopping away, springing through the near night toward who knows where.

Sister Laughs A Lot Mermaid took the bell back to the Sanctuary and told the Old Ems all about it. She put it on a string. If anyone ever forgot to laugh or was feeling joyless, Sister Laughs A Lot Mermaid gave them the bell to remind them.

It always worked.

And who knows? Maybe you have a tiny bell that can bring you and others great joy, too. Why not ring it and see?

Recipe

Make a Goddess

Over dinner one evening when the Sun had not yet dropped below the horizon, Sister Bridget Mermaid told the other Old Ems, "Annie Who Loves Birds told me a peculiar story about a divine being who was made from flowers."

"Why peculiar?" Sissy Maggie asked. "That seems perfectly correct: a goddess made from flowers."

The other Old Mermaids nodded in agreement.

"Her name was Blodeuwedd," Sister Bridget Mermaid said. "In one telling, she was created for a man who was cursed by his own mother never to have a wife. So wizards got together and created him a woman from the earth, using flowers. Nine flowers, to be exact. Some with names I've never heard before: primrose, bean, broom, meadowsweet, burdock, nettle, hawthorn, oak, and chestnut."

"Meadowsweet," Sister Laughs a Lot Mermaid said. "Ahhh. I like that name. They all sound so lovely."

"So this woman made of flowers," Sister Sophia Mermaid said, "she was made to be a wife?"

"In one story," Sister Bridget Mermaid said, "she was not satisfied in that role. So things did not end well."

"And in the other story?" Grand Mother Yemaya Mermaid said. "Do you like that tale better?"

"In the other story, she is an ancient goddess of the land," Sister Bridget Mermaid said, "who especially makes her presence known during the spring and summer when flowers begin blooming."

"I bet she's one of the Good Folk," Sissy Maggie said. "A woman made from flowers? It seems obvious."

"Yes," Mother Star Stupendous Mermaid said. "I agree."

"Next time we go out to Flat Rock Woman," Sister DeeDee Lightful Mermaid said, "we should cover ourselves in flowers. Perhaps we'll turn into Blodeuwedd and become divine flower women."

"I don't know about you," Sister Ursula Divine Mermaid said, "but I am already divine."

The Old Mermaids laughed.

The next time they went out to Flat Rock Woman, each Old Mermaid was covered in flowers—one way or another. It was spring, so there were not a lot of flowers, but they did the best they could. The Pepperwoman and Annie Who Loves Birds both had cloth with flower prints that they lent to the Old Ems.

> The next time they went out to Flat Rock Woman, each Old Mermaid was covered in flowers—one way or another.

One and all felt quite divine as they tromped out to Flat Rock Woman.

Recipe

- To prepare: Put your face in a flower or group of flowers first thing in the morning. It's best if dew is on the flower. Press your face against the flowers. Before you do it, check for bees, of course, and only do this in flowers where no chemicals have been used.

•Gather flowers. Only pick blossoms from plants that will not be harmed by the picking of their blossoms, and only pick flowers after you've asked the plants for permission and gotten it.

•Figure out a way to put those blossoms on your body, particularly around your face. (Blodeuwedd means "flower face.")

•Stand your ground covered in flowers. Breathe in the "essence" of these flowers.

•Feel yourself become a flower goddess. Yeah!

Recipe

Old Mermaids Treasure Box

If you'll remember from the novel, Myla Alvarez had a cigar box at the Church of the Old Mermaids every Saturday come shine or shine. It was there that she put some of her treasures; in this case, it was her money treasures which she used to help the migrants she sheltered at the Old Mermaids Sanctuary.

Cigar boxes have become a kind of symbol for treasure for those of us who wander in and out of the Old Mermaids Sanctuary. My young next door neighbor and I spent many afternoons decorating various cigar boxes and turning them into boxes that hold treasure.

After I finished writing *Church of the Old Mermaids,* my husband Mario and I wandered around the Lost Barrio in Tucson and ended up at our favorite art gallery (which is no longer there). It was chock-full of wonders, as usual. Every inch of the place seemed to hold some old beauty. I tend to get overwhelmed or overstimulated in those kinds of places, but Mario can find treasure almost anywhere. (A true Old Mermaid, he is.)

When I was about ready to leave, he came and found me, took my hand, and led me down and around to the back of the gallery. And there on a table was a cigar box with a mermaid strumming a ukulele on the cover! A cigar box with a mermaid on it that looked just like the one Ernesto had described in the novel. I was stunned. As soon as he was sure I liked it, Mario bought it for me. I carry it with me wherever I stay, wherever I go, and it is full of treasures that are meaningful to me.

You might consider getting a cigar box and decorating it. You could use it for all kinds of treasures. They're relatively easy to find. Go to a place that sells cigars and ask to purchase an empty box. They usually have scads of them. Cardboard ones are often two to four dollars, and the wooden ones are a bit pricier. They may smell like tobacco, but the smell goes away fairly quickly if you leave them open.

> May this box bring us treasures of good health and happiness beyond measure!

When you decide to decorate it, consider making a ceremony or ritual out of the process. If you've already got a sacred practice in place, you can follow that practice. I always honor the elements and directions, along with what is above, below, and in-between. I call on my helpers to join me. I ask the Old Mermaids to guide me in this process.

You could paint it or paste a collage on it. When working with the kidlet, we usually found pictures we liked and pasted them onto the outside of the cigar box.

You could leave the outside as is—because they are often beautiful—and do your decorating inside the box. Inside you could draw symbols from anything that has meaning for you.

When you're finished, you can bless it with your breath, run it quickly through a candle flame, sprinkle salt over it, and put a drop of water on your finger and press it into the bottom of the box as you chant a blessing and an intention.

"May this box bring us treasures of good health and happiness beyond measure!" You can mix it up, make it your own, change it all together.

Ingredients:
- Cigar box or other kind of box
- Crafting tools: paints, colored pencils, crayons, pictures to paste, scissors, glue.
- A sense of adventure!

Practice

Have fun. Laugh! Do things that bring you joy! Write about it or draw below.

Journaling

Dreams

Drawing

Mystery Six
Be At Home in the World

What does it mean to be at home with oneself in the world? Ahhh, that is the question. For some people, they are just full of themselves and at home everywhere from the get-go. The rest of us struggle a bit more. We struggle with who the culture tells us we should be, who we would like to be, and who we are.

Fortunately, age sometimes helps with this. Once we get a bit older—or a lot older—we say the heck with it: I yam what I yam. And then we get on with it.

Still, it is not unusual to feel as though we haven't quite lived up to whatever it is we are trying to live up to. It doesn't help that the world is awash in self-help gurus who assure us if we think the right thoughts or eat the right foods or do this, that, or the other, we will become happy healthy billionaires. "Why, look at Jane Smith whose house burned down while her husband was cheating on her, and she invented dippy-d whatever and she's a trillionaire who is happy as a clam living in one of her many houses around the world." How come Jane Smith can do it, and you get tired just hearing her story?

You get tired because it is not your story. (I wish Jane well, but what we've heard is never the whole story in any case.) We each have to figure out what our story is and who we are and then live it. So much is out of our hands. Part of being at home with ourselves is to understand reality. I have blue eyes. No amount of wishing or grumbling will change the color of my eyes. Now, if I really wanted to make it look like my eyes were a different color, I could probably get contact lenses to do that. I am five feet tall. No amount of wishing is going to make me any taller. In fact, I may even get shorter as time goes on! And there are things about my personality that are not going to change either.

Many of us have a complex relationship with the notion of home. I spent most of my childhood, right up to my teens, on a beautiful piece of land in rural Michigan. I knew every tree, every path, most of the animals. I understood the weather and the cycle of the seasons. I was absolutely besotted.

Members of my extended family owned land all around me. I spent my childhood on my grandparents' farm when I wasn't at my house. I roamed the hills, explored the river, had grand adventures in the forest. Then two things happened. First my grandfather died, and my grandmother couldn't run the farm by herself. My uncles and father helped, but they began looking for a buyer. Then my uncle sold the piece of land he owned next to our house. The person who bought it cut down my forest—which I had named the Lullaby Forest—and built a house. He also drained my beloved marsh. I was so devastated that I have blanks in my memory from that time. I thought I was going to spend my life on this land, and now it was gone. Eventually, after I left home, they sold the rest of the land, and now too-expensive houses dot the land where I used to run wild.

I spent decades trying to find home after those experiences. Away from that land, I didn't know who I was. Eventually I learned that I could more easily find home once I was more comfortable with myself—once I was at home with myself. Then I could employ skill sets that helped me be more at home with the world, wherever I was.

It's not always easy being at home with ourselves, especially if we're ill or locked in addiction or bad jobs or bad relationships. We can work and play at being at home with ourselves by incorporating the first five mysteries into our lives: Be here now; be full of yourself; embrace the wild; live your siren song; cultivate joy. In fact, if you've been living the first five mysteries so far, you might be thinking, "Of course I'm at home with myself and the world. Easy peasy." Yay!

> **Be here now; be full of yourself; embrace the wild; live your siren song; cultivate joy.**

It's important to be at home with ourselves when we're out in the world, too, not just when we're in our homes, by ourselves, or in the imaginal realms. We can serve ourselves and the world better when we are more at home in the world. The more comfortable we are with ourselves, the less likely we are to be reactive. Instead, we become thoughtful, mindful, and make better decisions.

Grand Mother Yemaya Mermaid and Tulip had a discussion

about this very topic as they were walking in the wash one day. The rest of the Old Ems and Tulip's mother were well ahead of them since Tulip and Grand Mother kept stopping to look at this and that. Tulip was a bit older then, not yet a teen but no longer quite a child.

"Grand Ma Yemaya," she said. "Do you ever feel lonely?" They were standing by a mesquite tree whose branches extended into the dry river a bit.

"Sometimes," Grand Mother Yemaya Mermaid said, "when I have momentarily forgotten what good company I am."

Tulip reached up to touch one of the rust-colored pods hanging from the mesquite.

"You are good company," Tulip said. "I am not such good company. I know all my stories."

Grand Mother Yemaya Mermaid laughed. "Yes, but you're always living new ones."

"I don't know what I want to be when I grow up," Tulip said, "or what I want to do."

> Up ahead, the group of women moved through the wash like a giant school of very colorful fish.

They began walking again. Up ahead, the group of women moved through the wash like a giant school of very colorful fish—out-of-water fish.

"Be the best you you can be," Grand Mother Yemaya Mermaid said. "That's all you need to do."

"What if being me isn't good enough?" Tulip asked. "Maybe I should try to be someone else."

"Is that possible?" Grand Mother Yemaya Mermaid asked. "I suppose you could be someone different than who you are, but why? You are you. No one else is you. That's an incredible gift."

"I hadn't thought of it that way," Tulip said. "Be me and live free!"

Grand Mother Yemaya Mermaid laughed again. "Yes! And if you feel lonely, remember the plants are always with you. Always. You are never alone."

> Remember the plants are always with you. Always. You are never alone.

"What if I were in the desert?"

"You are in a desert."

"One where there is only sand and sky," Tulip said. "No plants."

"Hmmm," Grand Mother Yemaya Mermaid said. "Then I guess you and the sand will have to come up with some new stories. Remember, sand is the skin of the Earth. Earth is your home. This is where you belong."

"What if I went to live in the stars," Tulip asked. "Would Earth still be my home?"

"You would still be your home," Grand Mother Yemaya Mermaid said. "Wherever you go, you will still be at home."

Tulip tapped her chest. "Home." She smiled. "Yes. That feels right."

Menu for the Tea Shell

Singing Up the Sun Tea
To Drink Before the Singing

Who-Who-Who Are You Tea
Recipe from the Great Horned Owl

Black As Night Bean Soup
Served with Hot As the Sun Salsa
Especially good during New Moon

Tiny Tortilla Soup with Tiny Tortillas
Recipe left By the Good Folk

See Weed Soup
With Sister Ruby Rosarita Mermaid's
Special Bread, Served with Butter from
the Cow Jack Tried to Trade for Magic Beans

Tale

Sister Ursula Divine Mermaid and Kadar's Shed

It happened one summer that Riya and Kadar's shed burned down, the one with Kadar's murals on the inside, along with her art supplies. All the Old Mermaids and most of the neighborhood went down the wash and then up over the ridge to help them build a new shed. Only when they got there, Riya was gone, and Kadar was bereft.

"Where is Riya?" Mother Star Stupendous Mermaid asked. "Has she gone to get more supplies? We have plenty."

Kadar stood on the porch of their house and shook her head. She did not look like herself. Sister Ursula Divine Mermaid wondered how her eyes had gotten so glassy.

"She said the fire burned away her desire to be here," Kadar said. "She wants to be somewhere cooler and wetter. I told her I would go with her, but she didn't want me." She whispered. "She didn't want me."

"What can we do?" Sister Sheila Na Giggles Mermaid asked. "We're ready to build you a new shed."

"I appreciate it, but I have no paints. I have no supplies. It all went up in smoke."

"You didn't go up in smoke," Sister Sophia Mermaid said.

"This isn't home without Riya," Kadar said. "Without Riya and art, I'm no better than smoke."

Sister Ursula Divine Mermaid was most at home where the wild things roam.

"Let us put up the shed," Sister Laughs a Lot Mermaid said. "So it'll be there when you need it."

Kadar agreed. Sisters Faye and Bridget Mermaids did a groundbreaking ceremony. They asked the Spirits of Here and Spirits of There for permission to build upon the ashes of the old place.

Kadar barely helped with the construction. With permission, the Old Mermaids went inside the house and prepared refreshments and snacks for everyone. With the help of Annie Who Loves Birds, The Pepperman and Pepperwoman, and others, the shed was up in no time. Sisters Bridget and Faye Mermaids, along with everyone else, said a blessing for the new building. Then everyone who had come packed up to go before dark.

Kadar stood staring at the shed, her hands on her hips, and she still looked completely lost.

Sister Ursula Divine Mermaid was most at home where the wild things roam. Like all the Old Mermaids, she was a good neighbor, and she helped out when she could. As she watched Kadar, she remembered when they had first come to the New Desert. Sister Ursula Divine Mermaid had been lost, hadn't been able to sleep, and had journeyed to see the Old Woman and Old Man of the Mountains where she got some wisdom from Old Bear and Old Sycamore and received her new name: Sister Ursula Divine Mermaid. She felt like she understood Kadar, so she decided to stay with her for a while.

On the first morning after the first night, Kadar said, "I've read every book I could find. I've listened to every advice that was given to me. Still Riya left. I don't know what to do. Can you help me? Do you want to take me on long hikes? Should I go up the mountains to see the Old Woman and Old Man? I'm ready."

"Just sit for a bit," Sister Ursula Divine Mermaid said, "with your bare feet on the bare ground. Then do whatever you want for the rest of the day and night."

Kadar took her chair off the porch and put it down by the shed. Sister Ursula Divine Mermaid began painting the shed.

Kadar said, "Riya told me she was going to leave so long ago. I thought I could convince her to stay."

Sister Ursula Divine Mermaid said, "Sit with your bare soles against the ground. You don't need to go over the past again and again. Think about nothing if you can. If you can't, think about how the earth feels against your feet."

"What if a scorpion bites me?" Kadar asked.

"Then a scorpion bites you."

"What if a rattlesnake bites me?"

"Then a rattlesnake bites you."

"What if the sun fries my skin?"

"You have lived here most of your life," Sister Ursula Divine Mermaid said. "This is your home. You know the answer to all of those questions."

"It doesn't feel like my home."

Sister Ursula Divine Mermaid didn't answer her.

Kadar moved her chair so that she sat in the shade of the

> **Sit with your bare soles against the ground.**

The Old Mermaids Mystery School **157**

shed, and she watched the ground around her feet now and again, just to see what was up. Mostly, she sat with her feet on the ground.

After a while, Kadar stood. "I'm done for today. How about lunch?" And she went into the house and made them a meal.

The next day, Sister Ursula Divine Mermaid painted more of the shed while Kadar sat with her bare feet against the earth. After a while, Kadar got up and went in and made them lunch.

This went on for several days. Kadar sat with her feet against the ground sometimes for a long while, sometimes for a short while. Once, she even fell asleep.

After Sister Ursula Divine Mermaid was finished painting the shed, she said, "This is now your canvas."

The days were hot, but most mornings Kadar and Sister Ursula Divine Mermaid followed a javelina trail through the desert. At first, they said little to one another. After a time, Kadar began pointing out things to Sister Ursula Divine Mermaid.

"There's a bobcat den over there, at the base of that tree," she said, pointing.

The jackrabbits gather over there during the full moon.

"Down there is a tinaja, in case you're ever here without water. There's always something there."

Kadar pointed. "The jackrabbits gather over there during the full moon. I've tried to catch them dancing, but I haven't seen it yet."

Some days, Kadar sat in the chair with her feet on the ground and wept.

When the monsoons began, Kadar stood outside and watched the water wash across her bare feet. She held her arms up and out, taking it all in. Sister Ursula Divine Mermaid thought Kadar looked like a wild woman. She nodded and went to stand beside her.

One morning, Kadar said, "I am ready to paint. I found some supplies in a closet the other night. Let me take you home, Sister Ursula Divine Mermaid. You can't walk the wash during the monsoons, of course."

And so Sister Ursula Divine Mermaid followed Kadar through the desert. They talked about everything they saw and what stories they had heard and what they hoped Sister Ruby Rosarita Mermaid was making for lunch. Sister Ursula Divine Mermaid was glad to see that Kadar's eyes were no longer glassy.

The Old Mermaids were thrilled to have Kadar and Sister Ursula Divine Mermaid back at the Old Mermaids Sanctuary. They ate a scrumptious lunch together, and then Kadar said she needed to head out.

"Can't you stay a while?" Sissy Maggie asked. "We want to hear all about Sister Ursula Divine Mermaid's visit."

Kadar said, "Thank you for your hospitality. And thank you so much, Sister Ursula Divine Mermaid, for all you've done. But now, I am ready to head home."

And so she did.

Practice

Be here now, be full of your true self, embrace the wild, live your siren song, cultivate joy, and be at home with yourself in the world. Enough said? Write and/or draw your experiences.

Journaling

Dreams

Drawing

Mystery Seven
Encourage Your Creative Process

For the first six mysteries, you have strengthened your footing in this world. With all of that under your belt—or soaked into the scales of your tails—you are ready to go deeper, to cross sacred thresholds, to embrace the Invisibles and our relationship to them, and to explore what it means to be an Old Mermaid.

The word "encourage" means "in courage." So the seventh mystery is about giving yourself courage to be creative and to trust your creative process. The first step is actually giving yourself permission to be creative.

We are all creative people. A woman's ability to give birth is the ultimate in creativity, but we are not talking about biological creativity here. You can be creative on how you live your life, how you dress, how you interact with people, how you do your job. You can also choose to be a writer, artist, photographer, designer. Remember, you don't have to be the best in your creative endeavors. You don't even have to be particularly good at whatever you are creating. It is the act of creation itself we are concerned with initially. It is about letting yourself step into that creative flow. Often, it is about letting yourself be uncomfortable, at least at first. From the initial discomfort of creativity, great things can come.

For instance, I am not very crafty. I am also a librarian who often worked with children. For years, I would not do craft projects because I knew I wasn't good at them, and I didn't want to publicly out my obvious deficits in this area. But finally, I said to heck with that: I am going to try it. And I did. I still wasn't particularly skilled at it. My creations looked like children's creations. So what? The kids did not care. As I let go of my ideas of perfectionism, my discomfort went away. I still get the occasional twinge of "I wish I were better at it," but I don't focus on that.

I love public art and creating community. A few years ago I came up with a project called *We Are Here: Geography of the Heart* where the community would create a huge map of our area on canvas. The library agreed to fund it. The plan was to have artists in the community paint the canvas first, and then the public would come in after and add story tags to the map (where they had written their memories of certain places). I had created and facilitated community programs for years, but I hadn't done anything this big before, in scale and in money. I was nervous. I wasn't an "artist," yet here I was daring to do public art! I was definitely out of my comfort zone. I knew if no artists got involved, I couldn't do the map: I was not an

> **From the initial discomfort of creativity, great things can come.**

artist, I kept telling myself. At least, I wasn't a trained professional artist.

After months of planning and weeks of publicity, the night came when the artists were due to arrive. I had written to dozens of them. I had talked to others. I had all the paints, brushes, and water out and ready for them. I waited. And waited. Not a single other soul showed up that night.

> **I picked up a brush and began to paint the canvas green.**

I was devastated—and sick to my stomach. What was I going to do? I couldn't do this project on my own. The canvas nearly covered an entire wall. I sat on the floor for a while feeling sorry for myself. Then once again I said to heck with this. No matter how amateurish it might turn out, I was going to make certain this project succeeded. I picked up a brush and began to paint the canvas green.

Fortunately, the next day about ten members of the public showed up, and we all just began painting our memories onto the canvas. It was an amazing experience for us and the rest of the public once it was finished. If I had let my discomfort get in the way, if I had given into my ideas of perfection, I would have never finished the map—and I would have missed a glorious time.

So work and play at opening up to the creative process. Educate yourself ahead of time—for instance if you want to create with clay, read up on it—but don't let that stop you. Don't wait until you can be brilliant at it. For one thing, you may never be brilliant at it. Eventually, just do it. For this mystery, the process of opening yourself up to creativity is the goal.

Opening ourselves up to the creative process also means that we are accepting and nourishing our ability to destroy as well as create. This is such an important concept. We have the power to create and the power to destroy. Destruction is part of the creative process.

> **We have the power to create and the power to destroy. Destruction is part of the creative process.**

A sculptor or woodworker chips away at the marble or piece of wood until she finds the shape she wants. She is essentially destroying what was—at least part of it—and creating something new. When I write a novel, I go back and edit. I am destroying what was to make the creation better. We weed our gardens to make better gardens. We cut away fabric to make a shirt. We destroy as we create. I encourage you to come to terms with your abilities as creatrix and destroyer.

Remember, when we create, we are becoming mediators between here and there. We become the sacred threshold, the in-between place. We envision something . . . else . . . and then we bring it from our imagination, from the ether, to *here*. How powerful is that?

How do you encourage your creative process? Explore different modes of creativity. If you normally paint, why not sew something or write a poem? If you normally write, try painting or drawing. Do something different. Let yourself be purposely uncomfortable.

Participating in activities which are initially uncomfortable is part of creating an agile mind. We need creative solutions to today's problems—so we need agile minds! When we learn to step out of our comfort zones, we can participate more fully in our communities and in our own lives. Encouraging your creative process is part of that.

P.S. FYI: My book *Answering the Creative Call* is all about encouraging the creative process, and it has many ideas about exploring different ways to be creative.

Tale

Sister Bridget Mermaid and the Blessing Time

The Old Mermaids understood their world as best they could, and they lived the most artful lives they could, too. They believed art and life went hand in hand, or rather, art and life were one and the same. To be whole and healthy, one had to create, one way or another, although the Old Ems probably wouldn't say it like that. Most would shrug and ask you about your day or what the coyotes sounded like the night before or what dreams you had in the early morning hours—because those dreams are the most powerful ones.

Sister Laughs a Lot Mermaid's art was laughter; Sister Ruby Rosarita Mermaid's art was food; Sissy Maggie Mermaid's art was multifold: She painted, she created clothes, she loved everything. Sister Bridget Mermaid's art was words and music and friendship, and she knew how to celebrate. Most summers, she helped the Old Mermaids create their annual Blessing Dance.

In the summer, the Old Mermaids left the Old Mermaids Sanctuary during the Hottest Days. Like many of their neighbors, they traveled up the mountains before the desert got too hot. They spent their days and nights near their neighbors, amongst the fir trees, near Summit Spring. At night, they sometimes gathered at a small meadow to watch the stars and listen to the owls.

Sister Bridget Mermaid planned their Blessing Dance. That's what she called it. The other Old Ems thought of it as Sister Bridget Mermaid's Blessing Time. Because it went on for days—beautiful, lovely days.

Several days (and nights) before the Full Moon, Sister Bridget Mermaid would begin her blessings tour. At sunrise, often after they sang up the Sun, Sister Bridget Mermaid would stand with her palms up and out, facing the Old Mermaids, and say something like, "May the love and affection of the Sun be on you. May the love and affection of these fir trees be on you. May the love and affection of the Old Owl be on you. May the love and affection of the dragonfly be on you. May the love and affection of this mountain be on you. May the love and affection of the New Desert be on you. May my love and affection be on you. All the days and nights for now and forever."

Sister Magdelene Mermaid or maybe Sister DeeDee Lightful Mermaid would say something like, "Ahhh, it's like beginning the day with spindrift in your wake. Lovely."

> **At night, they sometimes gathered at a small meadow to watch the stars and listen to the owls.**

At night, before the stars came out, Sister Bridget Mermaid might say something like, "May the power of the stars be yours. May the power of great dreams be yours. May the depth of the trees be yours. May the peace of the mountain nights be yours. May the power of the

The Old Mermaids Mystery School

great bear be yours. May the perspective of the eagle be yours. May all the protection in the world be yours."

Sometimes at midday Sister Bridget Mermaid would have a blessing for them. The neighbors came from far and wide to sit on the ground, close their eyes, and let the blessings flow.

"May the love and affection of the hummingbirds be yours," Sister Bridget Mermaid said. "May the love and affection of the poppies be yours. May the love and affection of the bobcats be yours. May the love and affection of the faeries be yours. May the love and affection of all the Old Mermaids be yours."

But everyone's favorite blessing was the Old Sea Blessing. It was a blessing that had been handed down through time, from mother to daughter, from mother to son, from father to daughter and father to son, forever, although some of the words were changed to fit the place and time.

Everyone's favorite blessing was the Old Sea Blessing.

One year on a late afternoon before the Full Moon rose, Sister Bridget Mermaid stood before the Old Mermaids and the neighbors. She took a deep breath and then let it out, loudly. And then she said, "The Old Sea and the New Desert send to you the deepest blessings to sooth every aching heart and every weary bone.

"The New Desert sends the songs of a mockingbird to you.

"The Old Sea sends a summer shower to you.

"The Old Sea sends the winds from the east to you.

"The New Desert sends the winds from the south to you.

"The Old Sea sends the winds from the west to you.

"The Old Sea sends the winds of the north to you.

"The New Desert sends the healing red of the penstemon to you.

"The New Desert sends the healing black of the crow to you.

"The New Desert sends the healing green of the palo verde to you.

"The Old Sea sends the healing blue of the sky to you!

"The Old Sea sends the peace of flowing streams to you.

"The Old Sea sends the peace of the cooling breezes to you.

"The New Desert sends the peace of the quiet mountain to you.

> **It was a love fest that went on and on.**

"The Old Sea sends the peace of the stars, moon, and sun to you.

"Great abiding peace of the Old Mermaids, the New Desert, and the Old Sea to you.

"The Old Sea and the New Desert send you this and more. Love, love, love."

They all stayed in silence for a time, until the Old Owl interrupted or maybe a child sneezed or laughed, and then the blessings began in earnest.

Nearly everyone stood and began showering blessings and gratitude onto everyone else, including the trees, bees, and fleas. It was a love fest that went on and on. When the Full Moon came up and turned its light on the Meadow, the group began to dance and sing. They held hands and wandered the meadow performing the Water Dance, usually with Sister Bridget Mermaid in the lead, their dance becoming the model for the water to follow, to fill up streams, catchments, tinajas, arroyos.

Soon enough, it would be time to come off the mountain, to prepare for the monsoons. The Old Mermaids and neighbors always brought back with them hearts and souls full of Old Mermaids and New Desert blessings.

The Old Mermaids Mystery School

Wisdom

Old Mermaid Blessing

To be a poet is to be a healer, a shaman. Words are powerful. They can create magic or hurl curses. Words can put someone at ease or make them ill at ease (dis-eased). Words can help us lift the veil or they can build walls.

Write your own "Old Sea and New Desert" blessing. This blessing is modeled on a powerful ancient Celtic prayer for peace and healing that is sometimes called the "deep peace blessing." Celtic poets were mediators between Nature and humans. Be like a Celtic poet: You choose what parts of Nature you want to incorporate into your own Old Mermaid or deep peace blessing by picking qualities from the natural world where you live.

> **You choose what parts of Nature you want to incorporate into your own deep peace blessing.**

For instance: "Deep peace of the industrious beaver on you. Deep peace of the vast ocean on you. Deep peace of the ever-changing Mount St. Helens on you."

In the Celtic tradition—and in the Old Mermaids tradition—

saying hello and goodbye are threshold moments. They are sacred moments. They are perfect times for blessings and good wishes. Write a "love and affection" greeting, and then use it on someone. "May the love and affection of all your Ancestors be on you. May the love and affection of a kitten be on you. May the love and affection of the faeries be on you." Something along those lines.

> **May the power of the bear be on you.**

Write a "power" greeting, and then use it on someone. "May the strength of the old oak be on you. May the perspective of the eagle be on you. May the power of the bear be on you. May the fierceness of the hummingbird be on you."

Say them out loud again and again. Feel their truth and power.

Practice

Make Yourself into an Old Mermaid

This mystery is about encouraging the creative process. In other words, it is about recognizing the artist in you. So guess what? You are going to do some art. No argument. Do this. No one else needs to see it. But do it for yourself.

Make yourself into an Old Mermaid, artistically. Do it whatever way you want. With or without tails. Dress as an Old Mermaid and take a photograph. Do a collage of yourself as an Old Em: Take a photo of yourself and print it; then find a mermaid's tail somewhere and paste it onto your photo. Or figure out a different way to make yourself into an Old Em. It is your choice.

Have fun with it. Be outrageous. Or not. As you're doing it, or preparing to do it, think about what it means to be an Old Mermaid, but more specifically, how would you be an Old Mermaid, with your talents, your gifts, your siren song, you being full of your glorious self?

Practice

1. Create your own blessings.

2. Make yourself into an Old Mermaid.

3. Relax and have fun!

Journaling

Dreams

Drawing

Mystery Eight
Make Magic

What is magic? When I was younger, I thought making magic meant performing tricks and illusions the way magicians practiced their trade. If someone had asked me if I believed in magic beyond that, I wouldn't have known what they were talking about. Then when I was in my thirties, I read the nonfiction book *Drawing Down the Moon* by Margot Adler.

Adler wrote about people all over the United States who worshiped Nature and believed they could influence their environment with their words and actions: They made magic. I got goosebumps of familiarity as I read this book. It was the first time I realized other people in the world felt about Nature the way I did. And to learn they actually called themselves witches and believed in magic was enthralling.

Reading Adler lead me to Z. Budapest, Starhawk, Merlin Stone, Marija Gimbutas, Luisa Teish, and Vicki Noble. It led me to women who called themselves witches for various reasons.

Some of them called themselves witches because they were able to step into the natural flow and tweak it. Some called themselves witches to honor those women who had been historically accused of performing magic, of consorting with the devil, and who were then murdered by the church.

During this time, I learned about ritual, ceremony, and spells. I had become "chronically" ill by then, and the idea that I—a writer, no less—could string together certain words to create some kind of miraculous healing recipe and get well was tantalizing. Ritual, ceremony, and even "spells" helped me reconnect with Nature and myself. But as far as healing what ailed me physically, I found no magic for that.

For over 30 years now, I have studied folk magic and folk healing methods from all over the world. I have found practices which do help heal some physical ailments. I have worked with methods that can connect us deeply with each other, the world, and ourselves. The most powerful magic I have ever encountered—the kind of magic that actually made a lasting impression in my life, the kind of magic that actually changed things for me—was the magic of changing my mind. That was transformative.

> **The most powerful magic I have ever encountered was the magic of changing my mind.**

Here's an example. After the oil spill in the Gulf of Mexico in 2010, I decided to return to school to get practical skills on saving the world. Yep. That was how I viewed it. I chose Antioch University in Seattle, and I went there for a weekend once a month for a year to work on a certificate of permaculture and sustainable food systems. It was not a fun time. I was older than most of the students, and most had started

The Old Mermaids Mystery School

school together, so I didn't fit in. I had no friends. We were supposed to collaborate online, but none of the other students ever wanted to do that. The traffic to and from where I lived and Seattle was awful. I felt like people were trying to kill me every time I was on the freeway, and I didn't feel well most of the time.

I mostly stayed at the Quaker House apartment in Seattle when I was going to school. (Many Quaker Houses in the United States have apartments for travelers. It's nothing fancy: a room and a bed, usually, and the price is good.) It wasn't my favorite place. A busy highway was almost directly overhead the house. The room was in the basement so it was always a bit damp. A huge male rat rambled up and down his own little trail just outside the window. And I was never quite sure what that big spot on the wall was from.

Near the end of the year and my time at Antioch, I lay in bed one night. I was exhausted. I didn't feel well. Mario was with me this particular weekend, sleeping in the twin bed next to me. I needed to get some sleep, but suddenly a light came on outside and flooded the room. I could hear two people talking outside, near my basement window. At first I thought, "How inconsiderate can people be?" I worried that I would never get to sleep. I couldn't make a scene, though. That wouldn't be neighborly, and I respected the Quakers and didn't want to jeopardize the apartment in any way.

> **Everything felt completely different than it had only moments earlier.**

I said to myself. "What if you were in another country trying to sleep? What if the light came on and two people began talking? You would just think it was part of the adventure of being on a trip to a foreign land. Later, you would remember the silver light in your room as the two people talked. You would remember the sound of their whispers even though you couldn't understand their words." As I thought all of this, I began to relax. I sank into my bed. I began to get sleepy. I wished I could hear what the people were saying. I wanted them closer and louder. Everything felt completely different than it had only moments earlier. But the only thing that had changed was how I felt about the situation. I smiled to myself. Ahhh, so this was what it meant to change one's mind, truly. Not long after, the voices went away, someone shut off the outside light, and I lay in the darkness, awed by my adventure in this strange new world. Then I fell asleep.

> **Often when people talk about magic, they are looking for a quick fix to transform everything.**

Often when people talk about magic, they are looking for a quick fix to transform everything. That aha! moment. And that happens. Sure. My experience—and the experiences of nearly every spiritual teacher I've studied with—is that those seemingly instantaneous enlightenment events either come after many years of study or they happened but they don't last.

It's like when we go to a workshop or on vacation and everything feels better, deeper, transformed while we're there. Then we go home and everything feels the same: shallow and entrenched. This is because we still need to do the work, call in the magic, and do our practices. The workshop or the vacation showed us what was possible; when we go home, we need to help that possibility become a reality. That is true magic.

For the Old Mermaids, magic means many things. Magic is about transformation—the kind of transformation that happens when we change our minds. It is about finding beauty and delight in the everyday. It isn't about those jolts of ecstasy that come and then go, leaving us wondering why we can't feel that way all the time. Some of us keep trying to experience those "jolts" again and again. We go from one thing to the other to the other, believing that we will eventually stumble across the someTHING that will make us feel different, feel better all the time.

Some things do make us feel better, for a time. If we don't have a safe place to live, enough to eat, or good healthcare, getting all of those needs fulfilled will definitely make life better. But beyond those survival needs, making magic—transforming—and connecting is mostly an inside job.

So for you, dear novices, during this mystery—and all the days of your life—make magic. You figure out what that means for you. Is it creating ritual, ceremony, connection, healing, transformation?

For the Old Mermaids, magic means many things. Magic is about transformation—the kind of transformation that happens when we change our minds.

For Sister Ruby Rosarita Mermaid it was about transforming items (mostly plants) into dishes that delighted her sister mermaids and the members of her community. With each meal she created, she whispered and sang and chanted her love into each ingredient in the hopes of bringing nourishment and healing to everyone who partook. She took a seemingly ordinary task and recognized how profoundly magical it is. You can do that, too.

What does making magic mean for you?

Tale

Sister Ruby Rosarita Mermaid and the Sous Chef

From the Visitor's Log at the Old Mermaids Sanctuary:

This might be longer than your average comment on your log, my dear Old Mermaids, but I hope you'll add it anyway. Or keep it just for you. It doesn't matter. I want to say some things. Yes, my time at the Sanctuary was wonderful, as so many of your previous guests wrote in the log. (I read it before I left.) The conversations were funny and profound—and sometimes difficult to follow if Sister Sophia Mermaid and Sister Magdelene Mermaid began going down one obscure path or another, as so many other guests have mentioned. And the food was divine.

But I have more to say. I came to the Sanctuary with a particular goal in mind. I wanted a profound spiritual experience. I wanted the gates of amazing revelations to open and let me in. I wanted to be suddenly changed so that I had endless patience, was kind to everyone I met, and was wildly successful at everything I did. I came here so tired of struggling. I came here so tired, period.

You all asked me to help out Sister Ruby Rosarita Mermaid because of the fall celebrations. The days and nights had gotten a bit cooler, and it was harvest time. The whole community was coming to the Sanctuary for days of feasting, singing, dancing, and having a good time.

I was surprised when you asked me to help cook. I thought I would be sent to a mountaintop to contemplate the heavens, maybe with Mother Star Stupendous Mermaid at my side. Or maybe I would walk the wash with Grand Mother Yemaya Mermaid whilst gazing at the navel of the Universe. Or match wits with Sister Sophia Mermaid. I had hoped to learn the best spells and chants from Sisters Bridget and Faye Mermaids. But no. I was to help Sister Ruby Rosarita Mermaid cook.

Cook. Good grief. That was what I had to do in my parents' house. That was what I had to do in my own life, to keep myself fed. But it was . . . meaningless. Cooking. It was just one of those trivial tasks we have to do every day. I was certain I couldn't learn anything while cooking at the Sanctuary. I didn't believe I could alleviate my suffering by cooking or serving others what we had cooked. But I was willing to give it a try.

It didn't start out well. I was resentful. I expected more. I had come here full of high hopes. Instead, I experienced nothing out of the ordinary.

Even the sisters were disappointing. I know, I know. I thought every word out of their mouths would be perfect. Inspiring.

I wanted a profound spiritual experience.

Absolutely revelatory. It wasn't. They were passionate about some things, depending upon the sister. They got angry. They got sad. They were happy. Sometimes they were ecstatic. I thought, how could I learn from them if they aren't always patient, if they get angry? They are no better than me.

I helped Sister Ruby Rosarita Mermaid with the cooking.

Before we started one morning, she ran a piece of cloth under the water, wrung it out, and then put it around her neck.

"Ahhhh," she said. "Much better. Would you like one, too?"

"What for?" I asked.

"To help with the heat," she said. She was wearing a long cotton skirt the color of pomegranate along with a peach-colored shirt that morning. She had a droopy flower in her hair. I kept wondering what kind of flower could it possibly be in a place that was so desolate, hot, and flowerless.

She was claiming a wet cloth around the neck helped with the heat? That sounded impossible and stupid to me. I said, "No. I don't think so. I'm surprised you have to use it. I thought all the Old Mermaids were naturally acclimated to the heat."

Sister Ruby Rosarita Mermaid laughed. "Not exactly. Some of us are a little more comfortable in the heat than others. But this kitchen gets very hot." She tapped the cloth hanging around her neck. "And this is a touch of magic that helps me through the day."

> Sister Ruby Rosarita Mermaid kept singing, "Beans, beans, we're mermaid queens. Make yourself the best we've ever seen."

We boiled beans that first day, if I remember correctly. Sister Ruby Rosarita Mermaid kept singing, "Beans, beans, we're mermaid queens. Make yourself the best we've ever seen."

She said to me, "As every wise woman everywhere knows, you always talk to the food, just as you always talk to the plants the food comes from."

She had a little poem or song for every part of the process. And she delighted in it all. Except when she didn't. She complained about the heat now and again, threatened to strip herself naked and cook that way, or find her way back to the Old Sea and jump in. I kept thinking if she were truly enlightened, if she were truly a wise person, she would not complain. She would not be hot. I was hot. I was miserable, but I was not an enlightened person.

She talked to her spoon, too. I am not joking. She would say things like, "Spoon, spoon, by this afternoon help us create a bean boon." Or rice boon. Vegetable boon. Whatever we were cooking. Her chants were always corny, always bad poetry.

She would laugh, sometimes kiss the spoon, and then dip it into whatever we were cooking after she sang.

She always had something cooking on the stove besides what we were making for the celebration, usually a pot of stew or soup she called the Never Too Many Cooks Soup or Stew. It started out with a pot of water. "From water we come, to water we return," Sister Ruby Rosarita Mermaid would say. She would glance over at me and shrug. "Once a mermaid, always a mermaid."

People were in and out of the kitchen all day. One day Old Neighbor Woman stopped by, tasted the water, and said, "Oh my. Delicious. But wouldn't it be even better with some of my carrots? They overwintered. And new onions. Some garlic." And so we would cut up those and drop them into the soup.

Sister Bridget Mermaid came by with some Old Mermaid tears. Someone—maybe Sister DeeDee Lightful Mermaid—added a few drops of the Old Mermaids Elixir.

Annie Who Loves Birds brought pieces of fish and dropped them into the pot. "All the correct prayers and blessings were

> Once a mermaid, always a mermaid.

sung," she said. As we stirred the pot when Annie left, I asked Sister Ruby Rosarita Mermaid, "What are the correct prayers?"

"Whatever you say from your heart," she answered. "The words aren't as important as the intent. At least that is true here. Isn't that true where you are from?"

I thought about it for a moment, and then I said, "I don't know. We don't generally talk to anyone but other human beings."

"Oh." That was all she said about that.

Throughout the day, people dropped things into the soup that became a stew and then a soup and then a stew and then who knows what. Sister Ruby Rosarita Mermaid would stir, let it cook, and then taste. "A touch of salt, maybe," she would say, "to give it that tang." Or maybe, "A bit of laughter." And then she would laugh like some kind of mad woman—or someone who was really happy. More than once, she asked me to taste the concoction and see what it needed. I finally said, "Closure." She laughed. "I agree," and she put the lid on the soup. "Come and get it as it is!" she called, and so people ate from the pot for the rest of the day.

Often we went out to the walled garden. Somehow she had made a little garden of Eden in the desert. When I asked her how, she said, "Oh, just a few ingredients in the right proportion. Like seeds, earth, water, sun. Have you ever looked at a seed, really? Have you ever thought about it?"

We were crouched near the ground picking lettuce or some other kind of greens. Shade from several pomegranate trees fell over us. I could smell dirt and something tangy or fruity. I couldn't quite place it. I balanced on one of my hands with my palm pressed against the kitty litter-like dirt. It was the first time since I had gotten there that I wasn't immediately worried that a scorpion or rattlesnake was going to sneak out of somewhere and get me.

"What about a seed?" I asked.

"Everything is in that seed," she said. "Everything is in it to become a tree, for instance. Or lettuce. Or a fig tree that grows figs. It has its own recipe. Right in that seed. It's miraculous. It's utter magic."

"That's just science," I said.

She nodded. "Of course. And magic. I once asked Sister Sophia Mermaid what the root meaning of magic was. You know, because words are like plants. They have roots, too." She grinned. Our basket was full so we stood and stayed in the shade for a few moments, talking. "She told me it meant harnessing natural forces to create marvels. That's science. It's about transformation. I mean, think about cooking. Wow. I was so fortunate that I discovered cooking when we came to the New Desert. Some of the other Old Mermaids had trouble adjusting. I never did. I had a purpose. I had to keep us nourished. The Old Neighbors—especially the Witch from Coyote Hill—helped me. In the Old Sea, *we* were magic. Us. Our bodies. Here we have to create magic or recognize it. We're different here. Everything is different. It's as if everything before we got to the New Desert was a dream, without consequence, and now we're here and everything is consequential. I mean, I can change my mind about something and everything suddenly changes. Or nothing changes except me. I'm in a constant state

Words are like plants. They have roots.

The Old Mermaids Mystery School

of transformation here. I watch it every day: I take ingredients, put them together, say a few words, and voila! we have a transformation. We've created a new thing. A new dish. I am a magician! Ta da!" She put her arm up into the air. "That is so amazing to me."

"Cooking seems so ordinary," I said to her. "We do it every day."

"Isn't that grand?" she asked. "We make magic constantly in this new world. I love that."

I had never thought about cooking like that before. I hadn't thought about anything like that before. I couldn't think about it any longer because it was time for the celebrations. We finished cooking the rice, beans, and putting together several casseroles. We set the food out by that strange pool. The neighbors all brought dishes, too. We had music, dancing, and tall tales, as well as food.

At some point I had to run back into the house for something, and I stopped on my way to the kitchen, noticing the murals on the walls. I mean, I had seen them before but I had thought of them as amateur attempts at art. Now the mountains were familiar—yes, there was the north crevice and that copse of trees. Perfect. And the ocean scenes. Ahhh, the dolphins the sisters spoke about so fondly. The sea stars that reflected the night sky. I could almost hear the waves as I stared at the blue-green world. And the wash painted on the walls, barely discernible from the walls themselves. I felt something bubbling up inside me as I looked at it. I could feel the magic of it in my

> I could almost hear the waves as I stared at the blue-green world.

bones. How the wash transformed every year from something akin to a ditch into a creek and then a river and then back again. How powerful to cross those thresholds again and again—to be able to change like that was wondrous.

When I went into the kitchen, everything seemed to glow or pulse. As if it had all come alive during the minutes I had been outside. But no, that wasn't what happened. It hadn't changed: I had. I laughed as I stirred the soup. It smelled divine. Why had I thought it smelled like rotten cabbage? For a moment, I wondered which was true: Did it smell divine or like rotten cabbage? Could both be true? Yes! Maybe not rotten cabbage. Maybe divine cabbage. That idea made me giggle.

> Maybe not rotten cabbage. Maybe divine cabbage. That idea made me giggle.

I grabbed the spoons Sister Ruby Rosarita Mermaid had asked me to get, and then I went back to the party. I wanted to hear the stories. I had a few of my own to tell.

Some days later, I left the Old Mermaids Sanctuary and returned home. Everything felt dull again. Then I remembered what Sister Ruby Rosarita Mermaid had done most mornings: She went outside and stood on the bare earth; she sang up the sun; she talked to plants in the garden, to the clouds in the sky, to the blue door; she sang chants to the dishes she prepared. I began doing the same, only I did it my way. And everything changed, except that which stayed the same.

I wanted to write this to you, I wanted to share all this, to tell you I understand magic now. I understand transformation. I see beauty. I see ugliness. I see situations that must be changed. I see things that need to stay the same. Sometimes I know what to do.

Sometimes I do not. Sometimes I am angry. Sometimes I am sad. Often I am happy. More often I am filled with love and awe. Wow. Wow. Wow. I feel like a magician, a real live magic-maker.

Old Mermaids, thank you for teaching me to cook.

Recipe

The Magic of Blueberry Omelets

Best Blueberry Omelet for Friends and Family to Experience Magic

This is one of Sister Ruby Rosarita Mermaid's most famous breakfasts—although you can have it for dinner, too. Every ingredient means something to the Old Ems. They don't take anything for granted, and they are in deep gratitude for everything they use. This recipe came into being one summer when everyone and their mother brought berries into the Old Mermaids Sanctuary, and everyone and their father brought eggs into the Sanctuary. Sister Ruby Rosarita Mermaid had to do something, and she thought, "Who doesn't love an omelet?" (Actually, not all the Old Ems eat eggs, so if you don't either, just skip all the egg stuff and have a handful of berries.)

You can make this magic omelet any way you want. Put some scrambled eggs in the pan and add blueberries and then flip them over or put them in the oven like a frittata. Sister Ruby Rosarita Mermaid likes doing it by the oven method because she loves the beauty of it. The egg whites fold into the egg yolks and create a bright beautiful yellow mixture, and then it stays all puffy in the pan as it bakes. It looks lovely.

Also, you decide whether you want it more savory or more sweet. If you want it savory, leave off the honey/syrup and cinnamon. If you want it sweeter, keep that in.

Recipe for Blueberry Omelet

Ingredients:
- 4 eggs
- pinch of sea salt
- less than a pinch of black pepper
- 1/2-1 tsp freshly ground (if possible) cinnamon
- 1 tb of honey/maple syrup
- juice of half a lemon
- olive oil or butter or coconut oil
- 1/2 cup fresh or frozen blueberries (or other berries)

Instructions:
1. Preheat oven to 375°.

2. Separate the egg yolks from the whites and put in separate mixing bowls. Beat whites by hand until firm and fluffy.

3. Add salt, pepper, honey, lemon juice, and cinnamon to egg yolks and mix until smooth.

4. Carefully whisk about a third of the egg whites into the egg yolk mixture. Then gently fold the rest of the egg whites into the yolks.

5. Heat enough butter, olive oil, or coconut oil to coat the bottom of a 10-inch (oven-safe) skillet. Pour the mixture into pan and cook for 1-2 minutes. Then sprinkle berries on top of the mixture. Put skillet in pre-heated oven.

6. Bake for about 8 minutes and then check. Should be fluffy and set in the middle. May take up to 15 minutes. Watch so it doesn't burn, although it will brown on top. (If it's starting to burn you can turn the oven down to 350°.) Remove the pan from oven when it is done.

The Old Neighbors around the Sanctuary and the Witch of Coyote Hill told the Old Ems that blueberries sprinkled in front of their door would keep bad company away. Sister Ruby Rosarita Mermaid wasn't sure why that would be, but she always liked feeding the birds, so she didn't mind leaving berries around the outside of the house. Everything else in the dish—the eggs, lemon, honey, salt, and pepper—are all about drawing in love, good health, and prosperity, creating connection and being grounded, with a little spice thrown in.

Practice

1. Make magic—you decide how. Cooking, changing your mind, creating a ceremony, creating something spectacular.

2. Cook something from scratch. Use one of your garden plants if you have any. It can be very simple or very complicated.

3. Start thinking about ritual or ceremony. What do you like in a ritual or ceremony? What moves you? If you do ritual regularly, think about what you like and what doesn't work. If you don't do ceremony, think about where you've experienced ritual or ceremony before but haven't really thought about it: in church, going to a wedding, attending a ball game, etc. Start thinking about what you would like for your own Gifted Ceremony.

Journaling

Dreams

Drawing

Mystery Nine
Be Wise

This is the ninth mystery. You have come a long way. The changes in you may be subtle, or they may be obvious.

Once someone becomes exposed to or dedicated to the stories of the Old Mermaids, one begins a kind of slow soul retrieval. Shamans and medicine people all over the world believe that people can and do lose their souls or soul parts because of trauma of one kind or another. Sometimes that trauma is physical, sometimes emotional, and sometimes it's a kind of slow soul death when we ignore our soul's call to the wild—the call to become our true selves. The tales of the Old Ems can help us fit all of our soul parts back into our glorious bodies.

By now, the Old Mermaids may have each become a *soror mystica* for you—a mystical sister. In alchemy, a soror mystica was required for transformation to occur. To find the Holy Grail, create the philosopher's stone, turn lead to gold—either figuratively or literally—the alchemist had to partner with the soror mystica. The mystical sister acted as a kind of mirror, reflecting back the divinity of her partner. That is what the Old Mermaids do best, perhaps. They hold up a mirror to us, without judgment, so that we may see the wisdom in ourselves, so that we can embrace our own divinity.

Mystery Nine is especially auspicious because it signals the birth of wisdom, the birth of the novice stepping fully into her wise self, into her Old Mermaid self. You have learned how to be here now, how to work at being full of yourself, you have embraced the wild and are finding your siren song, you are cultivating joy and being at home in the world with yourself, you are encouraging the artist within to come out, and you are making magic. All of this transforms into "sophia."

The word sophia originally meant "cleverness, skill," but over the years it has evolved so that sophia now translates into wisdom. Sophia was an idea that later became a goddess—or later was represented as a goddess and still later as a saint. In some stories she is the true mother of Jesus. In still others, she is the Great Mother. For us, she is wisdom. She is that hard-fought wisdom that comes when we stop striving even as we continue practicing. She is that wisdom that comes when we realize not everything is in our power—not even our own bodies and minds. She is that wisdom that comes when we know when to fight, when to rest, negotiate, step back, step forward. She is the wisdom that lets us know we are wise, especially when we recognize we don't know everything and we will get many things wrong.

> **She is that wisdom that comes when we realize not everything is in our power.**

Sister Sophia Mermaid is wise and often cranky. She wants

people to catch up with her. She gets cranky when people are purposely ignorant or satisfied with the status quo. (Yes, Old Mermaids get cranky.) She doesn't walk on eggshells. She is who she is, and she never apologizes for it. It wouldn't occur to her. She doesn't sit around thinking "I am what I am." She is herself. And that, my friends, is being absolutely full of true wisdom.

You may not feel wise, but try acting as if you are.

By the way, if you haven't made yourself into an Old Mermaid (see Mystery Seven), I encourage you to do so now. See yourself as the full-of-wisdom amazing Old Em you are. This is part of acting "as if." You may not feel wise, but try acting as if you are. Try to embody wisdom. How would you carry yourself in the world if you were sophia? What would you do differently or the same? Your body becomes the physical form of wisdom when you bring sophia into your body—when you embody it. The practices in TOMMS help with that, and dressing up as an Old Mermaid and seeing how that feels in your body will also help.

Write about how you feel at the beginning of this ninth mystery.

_____

_____

_____

_____

Tale

Sister Sophia Mermaid and Victoria

As you know, many people visited the Old Mermaids Sanctuary. It was a place to be when one needed to rest, to re-create, to feel safe and accepted. It was rare that a person had any problems at the Sanctuary. I don't mean everyone was the same. No, not at all. Each person was her or his own individual self. But every once in a while, someone showed up who had completely lost themselves—lost their bearings. This was true of Victoria Margrave.

When Victoria came to the Old Mermaids Sanctuary, she was what some people may have called a sad sack. At least that was what the Pepperman said. The Pepperwoman said Victoria Margrave was having a difficult time seeing the other side of things. She seemed to be lacking some of that ordinary wisdom that makes life easier.

The Old Mermaids each spent time with Victoria. Sister Sheila Na Giggles Mermaid showed her how to root herself with the trees. Afterward, Sister Sheila Na Giggles Mermaid could have sworn that not only was Victoria not grounded, the tree seemed a little wobbly. (Sister Sophia Mermaid assured her that was not the case.)

Sister Bea Wilder Mermaid took Victoria out into the wilds, across the desert, and up the mountains. She showed her ways to embrace the wild in herself. Victoria went through the motions, but by the time they came off the mountain, Sister Bea Wilder Mermaid could have sworn the whole world seemed less wild. (Grand Mother Yemaya Mermaid assured her that was not the case.)

Sister Laughs a Lot Mermaid tried to laugh a lot with Victoria. But, as you can probably guess, after she spent time with Victoria, Sister Laughs a Lot Mermaid did not feel particularly joyful. She wasn't sure she would ever laugh again. (Mother Star Stupendous Mermaid assured her she would laugh again.)

Nearly all the Old Ems had some time with Victoria. It's difficult to explain what was not working, but it was not. Victoria was uncomfortable all the time, and she seemed angry that none of them could make this discomfort go away.

So the Old Ems looked to Sister Sophia Mermaid. Victoria had seemed afraid of Sister Sophia Mermaid when she first arrived. She cringed at Sister Sophia Mermaid's boisterous stories. Seemed pained when Sister Sophia Mermaid asked her a question, even if it was something simple like "can you pass the pepper?" You know Sister Sophia Mermaid: She stood her ground firmly and fiercely. Victoria displayed all the physical ticks of someone who was intimidated by Sister Sophia Mermaid even though she never said so.

Finally Sister Sophia Mermaid took Victoria to the Tea Shell

> **She showed her ways to embrace the wild in herself.**

to work with her, Sister Magdelene Mermaid, and Sister Ruby Rosarita Mermaid for a while. Victoria had a lot of questions.

"Coyote Laughter Tea?" she whispered. "Did you have to kill the coyote to get it? That is horrible."

"No, no coyote was harmed in the making of the tea," Sister Sophia Mermaid told her.

"What about the Wisdom of the Palo Verde Tree Whispered to the Night Tea," she asked. "Wasn't that something private between the Palo Verde tree and the Night?"

Sister Sophia Mermaid shrugged. "Out here, nothing is secret."

> **Truth often comes with a story.**

"That seems rude," Victoria said. "What right do we have to take another being's secrets?"

Sister Sophia Mermaid looked at her for a bit, and then she said, "Is that an unpleasant way to be in the world, when everything is so literal instead of symbolic or mythical?"

"There's truth and then there's truth," Victoria said. "I am in search of truth."

"I think you're mixing up truth with fact," Sister Sophia Mermaid said. "Yes, there are facts. And most of the time truth includes some facts. But not always. Truth often comes with a story. You need context."

Victoria stared at her blankly. "I want to argue with you, but I'm not quite sure what to say."

Sister Sophia Mermaid laughed. "Now, see, that was truthful. And factual."

Sister Sophia Mermaid took Victoria to the trees out back of the Tea Shell to pick some figs for dinner.

"Shouldn't we save some of these for the birds?" Victoria asked as they began to carefully pluck the figs from the tree.

"The birds don't need our figs," Sister Sophia Mermaid said. "But we do. We won't pick them all, however, so that we have some for later."

The birds don't need our figs.

"How do you know they don't need your figs?" she asked.

"Because the birds were here long before we planted this fig tree," she said. "They know where to get food. We have to be a bit more deliberate about it. Thus this garden."

"You always sound so sure of your answers," Victoria said. "To everything. Do you ever have doubts?"

Sister Sophia Mermaid looked at Victoria. Then she took a bite of the fig in her hand.

"Do I ever have doubts?" Sister Sophia Mermaid said. "About what?"

"Anything."

"Sure," she said.

"You never sound like you do," she said.

"And?"

"It's intimidating," Victoria said. "You sound like you know everything."

"Why thank you," Sister Sophia Mermaid said. "I do know a lot of things." She smiled. "I don't understand what you're saying, though. Why is anything I say intimidating? None of it is about you."

"Human beings have doubts," Victoria said. "They make room for other people."

"First, I'm not a human being."

"You are now."

Sister Sophia Mermaid paused, and then she said, "OK. What do you mean make room for other people?"

"Well, you're just so out there," Victoria said. "And you're so sure of yourself. So full of yourself. I could never be that way. So I feel less than when I'm around you."

Sister Sophia Mermaid stopped picking figs. "I think we have enough," she said. "Are you saying you wish I was less than myself? Do you wish I was less full of myself? Who would you rather I was full of? If you are intimidated by someone else's personality, that's on you, sister. I would never ask you to be less than yourself; none of the Old Ems would. Why would you want me to be less than?"

"I would like to be less like myself," she said. "I would like to be more sure."

"Whether you are less or more sure isn't on anyone but you. If you don't like the way you are, you are the only one who can change that. Why not be yourself instead of wanting to be like someone else? Why not want to be like yourself?"

"Whoever that is."

Sister Sophia Mermaid said, "You don't see a bird asking 'who am I,' do you? Except maybe the owl. But I'm sure that is a rhetorical question. I doubt the trees wonder who they are. The mountains don't wonder either, at least as far as I can tell."

"Are you saying I should be more like a mountain?"

Sister Sophia Mermaid said, "Ahhh, you would not ask a mountain to be less a mountain, would you? So why would you

> **If you don't like the way you are, you are the only one who can change that.**

want anyone to be less themselves just so you could feel more secure about yourself."

"I never thought about it that way," Victoria said. She smiled. "Right. I don't want a mountain to be less a mountain or a bird to be less of a bird. Why should I want you to be less of a Sister Sophia Mermaid? None of that has anything to do with who I am. Victoria Margrave. Full of my quivering unsure self." She dropped the fig she was holding into the bowl Sister Sophia Mermaid had brought out of the house. "Yes! That's me."

"Sister Goofy Wisdom," Sister Sophia Mermaid said.

Victoria laughed. "Oh, I like that. Sister Goofy Wisdom Victoria Mermaid. Full of myself."

> With every meal she created, she whispered and sang and chanted her love into each ingredient.

This was how Victoria began becoming full of herself and acquiring some wisdom along the way. With every meal she created, she whispered and sang and chanted her love into each ingredient in the hopes of bringing nourishment and healing to everyone who partook. She took a seemingly ordinary task and recognized how profoundly magical it is. You can do that, too.

May we all do that same every day.

Practice

Calling In Wisdom

This is one of Sister Sophia Mermaid's practices.

1. If you can, go outside. If not, this exercise can be practiced anywhere.

2. Take off your shoes so that your feet are bare.

3. You choose which direction you want to face for your beginning. Some people are more comfortable starting their practices in the North, others are more comfortable in the East. Your choice. For this example, we will begin in the East. Face the East where the Sun rises. Raise your hands over your head, place them in the prayer position over your heart, or just let them be at your sides.

3. As you face the East say, "May I gather wisdom from the East."

4. Turn to the South and say, "May I gather wisdom from the South."

5. Turn to the West and say, "May I gather wisdom from the West."

6. Turn to the North and say, "May I gather wisdom from the North."

7. Then say, "I gather wisdom from above, below, and in-between. I am wisdom in all directions."

You can finish the day the same way. You can go outside, of course, but I usually do this exercise next to my bed before getting into it. You can face the West, where the sun has set, or start in the East again. Your choice.

1. As you face the West, raise your hands (or not) and say, "I am wisdom from the West."

2. As you face the North say, "I am wisdom from the North."

3. As you face the East say, "I am wisdom from the East."

4. As you face the South say, "I am wisdom from the South."

5. Conclude with, "I am wisdom from above, below, and all around. May there be wisdom in all places."

You can play with the wording. You might want to start the day saying, "I am wisdom from the East." And go around that way. You can call in whatever you wish for your day. I often begin the day with "May there be peace in the North. May there be peace in the East." Etc. "May I gather healing from the East." And on. This is a very flexible and powerful practice.

How do you call wisdom to yourself?

Journaling

Dreams

Drawing

Mystery Ten
Love

Welcome to Mystery Ten! You have now completed two-thirds of the Mysteries. You have chosen beauty, you have chosen wisdom, you have chosen the Old Mermaids Way. Congratulations.

Although it is up to you whether you do the practices or not, of course, in this case, you will need to go on the journey/meditation that I will describe below in order to complete the Mysteries. You will see why next mystery.

It is time for you to travel imaginally to the Old Mermaids Sanctuary. If you've done shamanic journeying before, use that method to go to the Sanctuary. If not, just think of it as a guided meditation using my description below.

Find a quiet space, preferably indoors where you won't be disturbed. Have a notebook on hand along with a list of all the Old Mermaids. Prepare the space in whatever way makes you feel comfortable, in whatever way makes you feel as though you are stepping into sacred space.

If you have worked with a helping spirit or guide before, one who looks after you when you are in the Imaginal Realms or the Other Places, call them in and ask for their protection during this time and beyond. If not, ask the Universe/Goddess/God to protect and guide you and/or ask one of the Old Mermaids to take you to the Sanctuary.

You will be travelling to your own personal Old Mermaids Sanctuary. This will be a place where you can go for respite or advice. It is in the Imaginal Realms, and it will be just for you. For this first journey/meditation, your intention is to go to the Sanctuary and talk to the Old Mermaids. You should say this intention out loud and/or write it down.

When you are ready, you can drum or rattle or put on a drumming CD that is geared for shamanic journeying. The drumming or rattling helps put your brain in a kind of trance.

When you are relaxed, follow your guide—imaginally—out of the room and down into a dry desert wash. Walk for some time. Feel the sand beneath your feet. Listen to the stillness. Perhaps a bird calls out somewhere. Feel the sun on you. Keep walking until you see a green sign swinging in a light breeze. It's an arrow pointing to the left with these words painted on it: "Old Mermaids Sanctuary this way." Step out of the wash and onto a path made from flagstones. This path leads you and your guide through the desert.

> **It is in the Imaginal Realms, and it will be just for you.**

Walk past cacti. Maybe you hear a coyote in the distance. Perhaps a roadrunner crosses your path. Walk until you see a gate with a sign hanging over it that reads, "Welcome to the Old Mermaids Sanctuary." There is no fence on either side of this gate. It is just a gate in the desert. Your guide opens the gate, and you walk through it. Ahead of you is a beautiful adobe house. It is so much a part of the desert that you blink a couple of times before it comes firmly into view. But then you see some trees around it. And a blue front door seems to await you.

Almost immediately, that door opens, and out come the Old Mermaids. They welcome you by name. They shake your hand, hug you, ask you how you are, and invite you inside. You walk through the house with the Old Ems as they talk to you. You glance around at the murals on the walls; you walk through the house and the kitchen and out the door until you are out in the walled garden, where the natural pool shimmers and the vegetable garden thrives. You sit on one of the many chaise lounges. One by one the Old Mermaids introduce themselves to you.

Spend some time with them. Listen to what they say, but don't worry if you don't remember. Try to pay attention, but don't stress about it. Try to see them all, but maybe you're not visual, maybe you just hear them. If you're not sure if you've met them all, feel free to open your eyes and look at your list to see if you've met all 13. Ask them if they have any advice for you. Don't worry if you don't get any advice or if it's only something like, "Eat your vegetables." Once you've spent some time with them, thank them all and say it's time for you to return home.

> **They shake your hand, hug you, ask you how you are, and invite you inside.**

You and your guide will then return the way you've come. When you're back in your room (or wherever you are), clap your hands to bring yourself fully back and thank your guide. Write up your journey. Then open the circle. You can do this by thanking the spirits and beings who traveled with you and by thanking the directions and elements. You can do this by saying something like, "The circle is now open and unbroken." And then wash your hands and/or splash water on your face.

Do this journey at least twice more before going on to the next mystery. Get used to the place. Try to remember more each time. For Mystery Eleven, you will be

> **She sewed love into the cloth with every stitch.**

going to the Sanctuary with a specific request. For now, you are learning the landscape.

Now, once you've done it this way, feel free to change it. Or maybe you already did. I know some of you don't like the desert, so maybe your Old Mermaids Sanctuary is near the coast or in the jungle. Wherever it is, find it and travel to the same one once or twice more.

It is time for less words and more action. It is time for less words and more meditation. Sister Magdelene Mermaid is our guide through this mystery. Sissy Maggie loves everything and everyone, so she is easy to be around. Another one of her gifts is sewing. As soon as she got to the New Desert, she set to work to clothe the Old Mermaids and protect them from the elements. That was how she demonstrated her love for the Old Mermaids. She sewed love into the cloth with every stitch. For the Old Mermaids it is not about the words "I love you." It is about the action of loving.

With Mystery Ten we are stepping deeper into the Mysteries and deeper into our own true selves. Note that Mystery Ten does not suggest you "make love" or "be love." The Mystery is "love." The word love is a verb, and it is a noun. In TOMMS, each of the mysteries is an action and a way of being in the world. Be here now. Be full of yourself. Embrace the wild. Live your siren song. Cultivate joy. Be at home in the world. Encourage your creative process. Make magic. Be wise. And now: Love.

> **But loving isn't about being a martyr. It's not about being fake nice.**

The word love is rich and heavy in meaning. Volumes have been written about romantic love. Uncountable songs have been sung about it. You know the Old Ems well enough now to understand they are not interested in semantics: What is and isn't true love? Nope. Not interested. While romantic love might make the world go round, the Mysteries are not focused on that. It is about constantly loving the world. That constancy begins with ourselves.

This action of loving doesn't have anything to do with sacrificing all to demonstrate love to the world. Although some sacrificing might occur because that's just life. But loving isn't about being a martyr. It's not about being fake nice. It is often about being kind, i.e. recognizing that we're all kin. Loving isn't about doing things which make us look like we are loving people.

So what do the Old Ems mean by love? Mary Oliver writes, "Love yourself. Then forget it. Then, love the world." That is what the Old Ems mean, too.

Your task now is to love yourself. How? You have all the teachings from the first nine mysteries to call up and use. You've been practicing being full of yourself. You've been singing, living your siren song. The practices will enable you to naturally achieve compassion for yourself, and you will love yourself. Hopefully, the lovin' has already begun. If it hasn't, you'll need to act as if.

As far as I know, the Old Ems never ran into Rumi, but if they had, they would have definitely called him brother. He wrote extensively about love. He said, "Your task is not to seek for love, but merely to seek and find all the barriers within yourself that you have built against it." I am fairly certain Sappho must have been at least an honorary Old Mermaid, too. She wrote, "Love shook my heart like the wind on the mountain rushing over the oak trees." Yes. That's love.

It is important to love ourselves, to recognize our humanity and divine spark. And then as Mary Oliver writes, we forget it and love the world. It needs love. This does not mean staring moony-eyed over what we love, be it a mountain, a river, or a person. We demonstrate that love. Not to be noticed, not to be angelic or pious. Thich Nhat Hanh said, "You must love in such a way that the person you love feels free." I think the Old Mermaids go further than that. They love in a way that everything is more free. They honor and respect all that they live with and amongst. If someone or something needs help, they help. If a place needs protecting, they protect it. If a word needs to be spoken to make a situation better, they speak it. It is a way of creating a life lived freely for everything.

> **Love shook my heart like the wind on the mountain rushing over the oak trees.**

Tale

Sister Magdelene Mermaid and the Young Woman

Sister Magdelene Mermaid enjoyed her life. When they first arrived in the New Desert, Sissy Maggie cried, just as the other Old Mermaids did. She missed the watery depths of their life in the Old Sea. She ached for the beings they had left behind, particularly because she did not know if they lived or died.

But Sister Magdelene Mermaid did not stay in the past. Once they got their bearings, covered their bodies with clothes the neighbors brought, and built their house, Sister Magdelene Mermaid went about discovering what she could do to help out in this new world. She created art on canvases for a time, but she soon discovered she had a talent with threads and pieces of cloth. They seemed to talk to her the way ingredients spoke to Sister Ruby Rosarita Mermaid or the way the stars seemed to communicate with Mother Star Stupendous Mermaid.

She began piecing together clothing for the Old Mermaids. She knew their personalities, so she easily created exactly what each Old Mermaid needed and liked. Grand Mother Yemaya and Mother Star Stupendous Mermaids preferred long loose-fitting dresses while Sister Ursula Divine Mermaid, Sister DeeDee

Lightful Mermaid, and Sister Bea Wilder Mermaid wanted comfortable pants and shirts.

When the Old Ems had enough clothes for a while, Sister Magdelene Mermaid went out into the community to see what she could do there.

Now, before we go on, it is important to note that Sister Magdelene Mermaid enjoyed herself. She loved her creations. And she loved sitting out in the garden in the shade of the Old Palm, listening to the sounds of the desert, so quiet and different from the Old Sea. She loved the birds she encountered every day. She loved the hills and mountains and the wash. She loved the cacti and the palo verde and mesquite. She loved to eat and dance.

She loved.

The Witch of Coyote Hill was the one who showed Sister Magdelene Mermaid how to weave and sew. At first it was all mysterious to Sissy Maggie. It seemed the Witch of Coyote Hill spun gold from straw or thread from desert plants. And maybe she did. The first thing Sissy Maggie made on her own was a Mermaid Purse. She sang every sea chanty she knew and every spell the Witch had taught her to make certain the purse was filled with wonder. When Sister Magdelene Mermaid went from place to place, she often carried her Mermaid Purse with her—and people could hardly wait to see what she had inside.

> **She created art on canvases for a time, but she soon discovered she had a talent with threads and pieces of cloth.**

One day she stopped at Haruka's house and pulled out purple socks partly woven from threads gotten from the pair Haruka's

The Old Mermaids Mystery School

grandmother made (and the goats mostly ate). Haruka gleefully pulled on the socks, put on her shoes, and then ran around the house, singing, "Grandma, Grandma! I've got my soles back."

That same day, Sister Magdelene Mermaid dropped off a baby quilt at the Begay's, one Grand Mother Yemaya Mermaid had helped her stuff with spider web batting, great horned owl dreaming, and duck down. Then they pieced together the quilt from cloth that in the end looked like a baby with two mermaid tails, one for each leg. Aponi and Bodaway thanked Sister Magdelene Mermaid as she wrapped the baby in the soft quilt. And then they ate lunch.

She dropped off scarves at a gathering of women who danced in the desert, most often under the full moon. To see if everyone was satisfied with their scarves, the women went out into the desert and danced for Sissy Maggie Mermaid. From far away, they looked like giant butterflies.

She had great conversations and accepted gifts of meals and hugs.

On her trek that day, Sister Magdelene Mermaid stopped many places and pulled out many goodies from her Mermaid Purse. She had great conversations and accepted gifts of meals and hugs. On her way home, she stepped into the dry wash to cross it and came face to face with a young woman. The woman stood in the wash, in the sun, dressed in winter clothes. She looked like she was about to faint.

"Hello," Sissy Maggie Mermaid said, "why are you dressed that way? It's summer."

"Dogs keep their fur all year round," the young woman said. "Why can't I wear my coat?"

"Of course you can keep your coat on if you like," Sister

Magdelene Mermaid said. "But you might die. This world is not an easy one. You can't bend it to your will."

"I hate the desert," the woman said. "And I hate summer."

"Why are you here?" Sister Magdelene Mermaid said.

"Everything I know is gone," she said. "This was the only direction I haven't gone yet."

Sister Magdelene Mermaid nodded. She held out her bottle of water to the young woman. "You need to drink," Sister Magdelene Mermaid said, "and you need to take off that coat."

> She held out her bottle of water to the young woman.

The woman took the bottle and drank from it. Then she asked, "Who are you?"

"I'm Sister Magdelene Mermaid. I'm heading home. You are welcome to come visit the Old Mermaids Sanctuary. We would love to give you a bed and meals. But you can't come if you're dressed like that."

"Why?"

"Because you'll die," Sister Magdelene Mermaid said.

"How can you live in this place?"

Sister Magdelene Mermaid shrugged. "We didn't have a choice," she said, "and now I love so much of it."

"I could never get used to it," the young woman said. She took off her coat and let it drop into the sand. Beneath it was a long wool dress.

Sister Magdelene Mermaid gasped. "How have you survived so long?"

"I wouldn't give in!" the woman said. "I will decide how I want to live! Nature can't tell me what to do."

Sister Magdelene Mermaid laughed. "I suppose not," she

said. "When we first got here, we had a very difficult time, too. But we couldn't go back. Can you?"

The woman shook her head.

"So maybe you could learn to love this place," Sister Magdelene Mermaid said.

"You are telling me I must accept the unacceptable," the woman said. "You are asking me to love what I hate."

"Maybe in time you won't hate it," Sister Magdelene Mermaid said, "if you give it half a chance."

The young woman made a noise.

Sister Magdelene Mermaid reached into her Mermaid Purse, but it was empty after her long day of wandering. So Sister Magdelene Mermaid lifted the hem of her little yellow loose-fitting dress and pulled it over her head. She held it out to the young woman. The woman blinked, and then she peeled off her very heavy dress and held it out to Sister Magdelene Mermaid who laughed again and shook her head. The woman dropped the dress onto the sand and took the yellow dress and put it on over her underwear.

She held out her arms and stretched. She loved the feel of the air on her skin. She loved the feel of the sun on her skin. She loved the feel of the world on her skin.

Meanwhile, Sister Magdelene Mermaid stood on the sand pretty well bare-naked except for her shoes and purple socks that matched Haruka's. She held out her arms and stretched. She loved the feel of the air on her skin. She loved the feel of the sun on her skin. She loved the feel of the world on her skin. She smiled at the young woman.

"You've given up all you have for me," the young woman said.

"I've given you a little yellow dress," Sister Magdelene Mermaid said. "That's all. Let's go this way. I know some women who are dancing on rocks. They have scarves that look like butterflies. I wouldn't mind wearing a butterfly scarf, along with the sunlight."

> I know some women who are dancing on rocks.

The young woman smiled for the first time. "This does feel better. And you are so beautiful."

"See," Sister Magdelene Mermaid said, "you've fallen in love already."

Practice

1. Become aware of your self-talk. It can be shocking to learn what you are telling yourself. If you are not encouraging yourself with every word you are saying to yourself, then change what you are saying. If you wouldn't say it to a 4-year-old, don't say it to yourself. As you rewrite and re-say your self-talk, make it an affirmative encouragement. For instance, if you've been telling yourself you are stupid (and that's very common self-talk), don't change it to "I am not stupid." Change it to something like, "I am so smart!" Or "Look at how bright I am. Yay!" Turn it into something that makes you smile. At first, these "rewrites" won't feel true or real. But after a while, they can be such loving boosts to your day. Exaggerate them. Make these statements into wonderful gifts to yourself.

2. Ground, sit quietly, and meditate on something you love. For now, do a place, thing, or concept, not people. Maybe you love the river or park near where you live. Or maybe you love something about your town or something in the Constitution of the United States. Big or small, meditate on this one thing you love (one thing at a time). Connect with whatever you are meditating upon. Ask it what it needs and what you can do for it. Don't stress over it. See what pops into your mind first thing. If that doesn't feel true, let that go and try again.

Maybe the Park tells you it's got too much garbage. Or maybe the River says they're spraying pesticides too close to the water. You love these places, but the idea of picking up garbage or asking the authorities about pesticides feels daunting. You don't want to do it. You've got too much on your plate. Now you feel resentful that you even asked. The whole world is just filled with takers. Now you're feeling stressed.

If that's your reaction, keep breathing. Let all feelings of obligation flow away. Keep breathing until all you are feeling is love for the place again. When you are feeling peaceful and loving again, ask yourself what you are willing to do for this place. What is too much, what is too little, what is just right? What action can you take which will continue to fill you with love? Work that negotiation out with yourself. Figure out what your ability to respond is, and then respond.

This may take some effort, but stick with it. Remember, the Old Mermaids weren't loving active members of their community because they thought they had to be. Everything they did was with love. If we are constantly doing things out of a sense of obligation that makes us tired or resentful, that's not good for anything or anyone.

> **Become aware of your self-talk.**

This doesn't mean we all don't have to do things we don't want to do. Far from it. But this practice gives you a chance to sort through what you really want to do as an act of love and what you're doing because you feel you must. Now you can change how you feel about your responsibilities and change some of the "must do" to the "love to do." And in the process, you will be able to let go of some of those things that are sapping your energy.

The Old Mermaids Mystery School

Write about your experience of this mystery.

Journaling

Dreams

Drawing

Mystery Eleven
Flow

Like Mystery Ten, Mystery Eleven can be expressed in one word: Flow. It's not about going with the flow, although that is sometimes what it means. Mihaly Csikszentmihalyi popularized "flow" when he wrote about being in the zone. To put it simply: When one is focused on a task, one is often happiest. From the perspective of the Old Mermaids, we flow when we live the Mysteries. Each one of the mysteries we've learned about so far helps us flow with life. Flow for the Old Mermaids was easy when they were able to be here now while also being full of themselves, living their siren songs joyfully, creatively, while embracing the wild, making magic, being wise, and loving. With all of that under their belts—and now our belts—focus does come naturally. Concentration comes easily. We can decide on a goal, focus, and work to achieve it. Flow is truly about the superpower of being full of yourself. Once that happens, doubts disappear; criticism goes unheard. You . . . flow . . . YOU.

You can achieve flow in your life by practicing all you've learned in the Mysteries. Specifically you can choose a creative task, focus on it, and complete it. We all know how to multi-task. That is what we do nearly constantly. Nowadays it seems more and more difficult to single-task. You can give your brain and being a rest by doing one task. Turn off your phone, your computer (or your wi-fi if you're writing on the computer), and your TV. Turn off all your devices, and then work or play. Do that one thing without being interrupted by any device.

See if you can carve out some time to flow without technology.

When I suggest this to women, many of them tell me they would never ever turn off their phones. "I have children," one woman told me. I replied, "Your children are grown and in their thirties." "Still," she said. For tens of thousands of years, parents were not in constant touch with their children. Didn't seem like the world would end if that woman turned off her phone for an hour or so. Or even 15 minutes. But she was not able to do it.

I turn off my wi-fi when I write. My phone is off most of the time. I know most people aren't willing to do that, but I do recommend trying it. It can be freeing. It helps you get into flow. My husband goes screen-free one day of the week (usually Sunday). See if you can carve out some time to flow without technology. See how it feels. For some of you, it will be extremely uncomfortable, at least initially. Try to keep it up until the discomfort transforms into something else. Most often the discomfort turns into the desire to do something. That's when you can focus on a task and see how you . . . flow.

In a different interpretation of flow, Sister Sophia Mermaid says, "Go with the flow and watch out for waterfalls." This is a warning about being too easygoing. In some philosophies, one is encouraged to just go with it. Don't try to stop anything because that's too much like trying to swim upstream. What the Old Mermaids understand is that we can't always go along to get along. We can be flowing down that stream, but we have to understand we will run into boulders, waterfalls, or shoals. In many instances in our lives, it is best to avoid the waterfalls, boulders, and shoals, but sometimes we have to step up and out of our comfort zones to right a wrong or fix a hurt. To the Old Mermaids, "it's all good" is meaningless (just as "it's all bad" would be meaningless). Because it's not either or. In their world, one fixes what's broken; one does not accept what is unacceptable; one maintains one's true self and flows with one's values. And sometimes that results in health and happiness for all, at least for a time.

Go out to a flowing waterway without any devices—or at least have them turned off. Stand or sit along the shore of this river (or stream). Watch it for a while. Be with it. And then imagine yourself merging with this water, safely, comfortably, and go where it goes. See if this practice changes or solidifies your view of flow.

Enjoy!

How can you start to go with the flow?

_____

_____

_____

Tale

Grand Mother Yemaya Mermaid and the Old Sea

When the Old Sea first dried up and the Old Mermaids washed ashore in the New Desert, they weren't quite certain what had happened. Perhaps they had gotten some hint beforehand that all was not well in their world, but they didn't understand what they could or could not do to prevent it or stop it once it started. They got no chance to say goodbye to friends, family, or any of the creatures of the deep dark Old Sea. The Old Mermaids were all that was left of the Old Sea for as far as any of them could tell. Grand Mother Yemaya Mermaid felt it was her obligation and duty to find a way home. But she could not see or hear the Old Sea; she could only feel it in her bones. And so the Old Mermaids stepped out of the wash, left their past behind, and built the Old Mermaids Sanctuary.

Some of the Old Mermaids had a more difficult time adjusting than others. Grand Mother Yemaya Mermaid did not always know how to counsel them, but she did the best she could. She had known all there was to know about the Old Sea, but here, what did she know of unrelenting sun and blue skies? What did she know of dirt and rattlesnakes, trees with spikes, and howling coyotes?

Although most of the other Old Mermaids didn't realize it, Grand Mother Yemaya Mermaid was a bit out to sea for a while once they washed ashore on the New Desert. She still gave advice when asked, but she was not quite certain what her place was in this new world. After all, in the Old Sea she was thought of as the great goddess who birthed everything. She rose up out of the water on full moon nights, huge, dark, and powerful, her two tails reflecting the moon in her blue-green flashing scales. Here she felt heavy: weighted down by . . . everything.

One night she went out and stood with Mother Star Stupendous Mermaid as she stared up at the stars.

"The stars here are just lovely," Mother Star Stupendous Mermaid said.

> She rose up out of the water on full moon nights, huge, dark, and powerful, her two tails reflecting the moon in her blue-green flashing scales.

"As lovely as they were in the Old Sea?" Grand Mother Yemaya Mermaid asked.

Mother Star Stupendous Mermaid laughed. "Of course. They are the same stars."

"I keep wondering what went wrong," Grand Mother Yemaya Mermaid said. "And I keep wondering why. But mostly, I cannot find the magic of this place. I miss all the wisdom of the Old Sea."

"I'm so sorry," Mother Star Stupendous Mermaid said. "I can see that it is difficult for you. I'm afraid my head has always been in the stars, so it's not that much different here for me, I suppose. But you are the deep blue sea. How lonesome it must get for you."

Grand Mother Yemaya Mermaid said, "I feel a longing for home that I've never had before."

"I do feel more awake here," Mother Star Stupendous Mermaid said. "Don't you? It's almost as if I were asleep before. And now I am awake. I have to pay attention to everything. It can be exhausting, it's true. But I love being awake."

Grand Mother Yemaya Mermaid pressed her lips together and thought about this. She supposed Mother Star Stupendous Mermaid was right. One had to be awake here: Injury and death lurked everywhere.

> One had to be awake here: Injury and death lurked everywhere.

"I sometimes return to the Old Sea in my dreams," Mother Star Stupendous Mermaid said. "You were always the best dreamer. Perhaps you can go for a visit in your dreams."

That night, Grand Mother Yemaya Mermaid set her intention to visit the Old Sea in her dreams. At first she had trouble falling asleep, but finally she was off to slumber land. Sure enough, she landed in the Old Sea. Once she got her bearings and her sea tails, she dove down deep into the water, going down, down, down until she reached a great green light, and then she swam past it until she found her mother, grand mother, great grandmother, and all the great Old Sea Goddesses. They swam together for a long while until they broke through the surface of the water to lounge on some rocks protruding from the Old Sea. The Oldest of Old Ems said to Grand Mother Yemaya Mermaid, "You may ask us anything."

Grand Mother Yemaya Mermaid thought about it for a bit,

and then she said, "Why has this happened to us? Why must we suffer this fate?"

The Oldest of Old Mermaids said, "We don't know."

Grand Mother Yemaya Mermaid sat stunned for a moment. How could a goddess not know the answer to this simplest of questions?

The room smelled of the Old Sea.

"Know this, daughter," said one of the Oldest of Old Mermaids, "you hold the Old Sea and all the wisdom of the Old Sea in you. And all the wisdom of the New Desert, too."

"Laugh or weep," one of them said, "remember that we are in your tears."

Grand Mother Yemaya Mermaid nodded. And then she stood—she had legs again—and she walked away from the Oldest of the Old Mermaids and the Old Sea. She looked back once but spotted only seals on the rocks. Then she opened her eyes, and she was back in the Old Mermaids Sanctuary—sleeping on soaking wet sheets!

Sister DeeDee Lightful Mermaid and Sister Magdelene Mermaid were standing at the end of her bed. Sissy Maggie held a bucket as she was trying to catch the water from the bed.

"You cried in your sleep all night long," Sissy Maggie said, "and made lots of water."

"And your legs flashed as though they were tails again!" Sister DeeDee Lightful Mermaid said.

Grand Mother Yemaya Mermaid nodded as she got out of bed, soaking wet. The room smelled of the Old Sea. Grand Mother Yemaya Mermaid pulled off her nightgown and took the bucket from Sissy Maggie. She held her nightgown over the bucket and squeezed the water out of it. When she was finished with that, she pulled off the sheets, twisted them, and watched the water drip into the bucket. Then she dressed, grabbed some cloth from a storage closet, along with needle, thread, and scissors. She took all of that and the bucket of dream water, and she went out into the desert.

Once she found a big flat rock near the wash, Grand Mother Yemaya Mermaid sat down and began to sew. She cut 13 long rectangular pieces of cloth from the various scraps she had grabbed from the closet. Then she took the ball of thread and dropped it into the dirt. "May this thread be imbued with the power, healing, wonder, wisdom, and mystery of the New Desert," she said. Then she dropped the ball of thread into the bucket of her tears. "May this thread be imbued with all the power, healing, wonder, wisdom, and mystery of the Old Sea."

After a bit, Grand Mother Yemaya Mermaid threaded the needle with the now-magical thread. She began to sew, turning the cloth into 13 scarves, one for each Old Mermaid. As she pulled the needle through the cloth, she sang and whispered sea chanties and coyote howls and owl questions and hummingbird hums and waves rolling on sand into the cloth, along with the mysteries of the Old Sea and the New Desert. As the day wore on and became night and day and time stood still and carried on, Grand Mother Yemaya Mermaid sewed magic into the cloth. The more she sewed and the more she sang, the more she felt like herself again. She was no longer adrift.

> **The more she sewed and the more she sang, the more she felt like herself again. She was no longer adrift.**

Soon the other Old Mermaids came and sat with Grand

The Old Mermaids Mystery School **249**

Mother Yemaya Mermaid as she sewed and sang. They brought food and drink; they brought stories and songs. When she finished one scarf, she would drape it over an Old Mermaid and say something like, "Sister DeeDee Lightful Mermaid, I sewed into this scarf the mysteries and wisdom of the Old Sea and the New Desert. And the Oldest of Old Mermaids wants you to know that laugh or weep, they swim in your tears."

One by one, the Old Mermaids had scarves with mysteries and wisdom sewn into them, until only one scarf was left.

One by one, the Old Mermaids had scarves with mysteries and wisdom sewn into them, until only one scarf was left. When Grand Mother Yemaya Mermaid finished that one, she placed it across her own shoulders and said, "Laugh or weep, they swim in our tears." And then Grand Mother Yemaya Mermaid looked around at the Old Mermaids, at the rocks, the empty wash, the blue blue sky. She listened and was quite certain she heard the Old Sea, if only for a moment, and then the pulsing stillness of the New Desert. She nodded. At least for now in this moment, all was right with her world.

Practice

Visiting Your Old Mermaids Sanctuary

You have by now journeyed to your Old Mermaids Sanctuary. (See Mystery Ten.) Prepare to journey to your Sanctuary again. This time your intention will be to ask the Old Mermaids for gifts for you for your Gifted Ceremony (which we will discuss in more detail in Mystery Twelve). Make certain you have the list of Old Mermaids and pen and paper to write down what the Old Ems say.

Create your circle, call upon your guide/protector to accompany you, state your intention: "To ask the Old Mermaids for gifts for my Gifted Ceremony." Then go on your journey to the Sanctuary. Once you are there, engage with the Old Mermaids. Ask them for their gifts and write them down. "I gift you with stories!" "I gift you with nourishment." "I gift you with Nature." They might gift you right away, but they may not. You may have to return several times. Try to get a gift from each Old Mermaid, but don't stress about it if that doesn't happen. Just journey to them until you feel it is done. Keep a hold of the list of gifts until Mystery Twelve.

Write about your experiences.

Journaling

Dreams

Drawing

Mystery Twelve
Honor the Ancestors

Ancestor veneration is something that happens worldwide in most cultures. Some of you already honor your human Ancestors. To the Old Mermaids, the Ancestors are everything that has come before them, not only their blood relations. The Earth was created from the Stars, and we humans are made of stardust. (This is actually scientifically accurate.) So the Stars are literally (as well as figuratively) our Ancestors. The tree that was hit by lightning and fell over last week is an Ancestor. So is the coyote who yipped her last howl a month ago. So is the good old neighbor who died last week.

When I first heard about honoring the Ancestors a few decades ago, I didn't really understand or appreciate the idea. First off, I didn't want to think about dead people. In my culture, no one called on the dead unless they wanted to be haunted. And who wants to be haunted? Also, I wasn't fond of any of the dead relatives I remembered. I couldn't figure out why I would want to honor them. (I was young.) As it turned out, I wasn't the only one who was hesitant to honor their Ancestors, especially if those dead relatives had been abusive in some way when they were alive. Many of my friends felt the same way.

Fortunately my view of "honoring the Ancestors" changed as time went on. For one thing, I realized that all of my human Ancestors did the best they could to survive. Without them, I wouldn't be here. So I stopped judging them. Also my idea of what constituted an Ancestor changed and aligned with how the Old Mermaids felt about the Ancestors. Once I thought of the Old Oak as being my relative and all the oaks who had gone before the Old Oak as my Ancestors, *mi familia* expanded to include the whole world. Once I opened up my view of my relations, as it were, I felt more at home wherever I went.

When we are able to embrace the idea that we are "related" to the entire Universe, we are set free, finally, from familial expectations. "Oh, I did not fit into my human family, but wow, I can definitely relate to the trees in a forest." Or, "Yes, looking up at this night sky, I know I belong." "I am quite certain my relatives were cats (or bears or dolphins)."

> **It is important to remember in this process that although we venerate our human Ancestors, too, it is not about living our lives for them or doing what they wanted us to do when they were alive.**

You get to choose how you want to honor the Ancestors, of course. Many people set up an altar for their Ancestors. Some people put up photos of their relatives around the house. It is important to remember in this process that although we venerate our human Ancestors, too, it is not about living our lives for them or doing what they wanted us to do when they were alive. Instead it is a way of acknowledging that we are not alone, and we did not get where we are on our own.

If you like, set up an altar to honor all your Ancestors, or write a poem to them. Or continue your conversation with the world around you as a way to honor them. It's your choice. The poem below is one of the ways I chose to honor my Ancestors—and define who an Ancestor is to me. (Those of you who have read and/or celebrated *The Salmon Mysteries* have already seen this poem.)

Invocation to the Ancestors

O my Ancestors
Upon your ashes I walk through life
Upon your dust I shall one day rest

O my Ancestors
You who flew above the Earth
You who burned with Passion
You who made your home in the Ocean
You who burrowed deep into the Earth

O my Ancestors
I ask for your blessings
And thank you for my life

Ashes to ashes
Dust to dust
All my relations
O my Ancestors

Tale

Mother Star Stupendous Mermaid and the Night Sky

Mother Star Stupendous Mermaid loved being outside beneath the night sky. For her, nothing was as satisfying as staring up at the stars. She felt as though she was viewing millions of her beloveds—or billions of her Ancestors.

Sister Ursula Divine Mermaid had made a wonderful lounge chair for Mother Star Stupendous Mermaid so she didn't get a crick in her neck—and so she was up off the ground, too. When Mother Star Stupendous Mermaid had been in the Old Sea, she had enjoyed finding a pool where she could sit above the surface and watch the sky reflected in the water. But nowadays, she loved being outside looking up, stretched out on the chair Sister Ursula Divine Mermaid had created. Often someone else watched with her, taking advantage of the second lounge chair Sister Ursula Divine Mermaid fashioned.

"What do you see up there?" Sister Sheila Na Giggles Mermaid asked Mother Star Stupendous Mermaid one night.

"For one thing, I see your face," Mother Star Stupendous Mermaid said.

"Where?" she asked.

"Over there, by that bright star," Mother Star Stupendous Mermaid said, pointing.

Sister Sheila Na Giggles Mermaid followed her pointing finger, and then she laughed. "You're pulling my tails."

"I am, indeed," Mother Star Stupendous Mermaid said. "But truly, I feel as though I can see the whole world here. Sitting on this ship we call Home and others call Earth, moving through the White River. We are going places and sitting perfectly still all at the same time. And we all started there, in the stars, and ended up here. Beautiful and impossible."

"Dearest Mother Star Stupendous," Sister Sheila Na Giggles Mermaid said, "I do believe you just summed it all up. Beautiful and impossible."

> **We all started there, in the stars, and ended up here. Beautiful and impossible.**

"Yes," Mother Star Stupendous Mermaid said. "Look. I think I see the Oldest of Old Ems up there, in that bend in the White River. Do you see them? I hope they're having as good of a time as we are."

"That hardly seems possible," Sister Sheila Na Giggles Mermaid said. "But they lighted the way for us, didn't they?"

Practice

Gifted Ceremony

This mystery is all about you creating a Gifted Ceremony for yourself. Like the one you read about in *Church of the Old Mermaids* when Poppy and Tulip were gifted by the Old Mermaids. All Old Mermaid children are gifted upon birth, a kind of goddessmother ceremony that guarantees each child is blessed from the very beginning.

Last mystery you journeyed to your Old Mermaids Sanctuary and received gifts from the Old Mermaids. You can incorporate the gifts you received from the Old Ems if you like. You get to decide how simple or elaborate you want your Gifted Ceremony to be.

Here are a couple of suggestions on how to do your Gifted Ceremony:

1. First, sit down and write out the gifts you were given on a sheet of paper. Then rip them off the sheet one at a time so that there is one gift on each strip of paper. Fold those up separately and put them in a bowl. Save them for later.

2. Next, decide if you want other people to be a part of your personal Gifted Ceremony. For now, this particular Gifted Ceremony is just for you. In other words, you are being gifted, no one else. (Next mystery, we will talk about Gifted Ceremonies for others.) If you would like family and friends to be a part of your Gifted Ceremony, that's wonderful. If you're more comfortable doing this by yourself, go for it. If you want other people to be a part of it, ask them to participate. Tell them they will be acting as if they were fairy goddessmothers/fathers coming to wish you all the best in your life. If you are doing it on your own, recognize that *you* are your own fairy goddessmother.

a. If you want other people to be involved, you might decide that you'll sit in a chair. You might instruct them ahead of time that they will each file into the room one by one. As they pass by the bowl filled with the strips of paper, they will each take one (or two) strips. Then one at a time, they will stand in front of you while you are sitting in your chair, and they will open the piece of paper and say, "I gift you with (whatever the paper says)." And then they will step back and wait for the others to gift you (or they could file out and get you another gift from the bowl—you decide ahead of time). As they're gifting you, try to feel that gift washing over and into your body.

When I've done this, I use a wand someone made for me years ago. I tap the wand to the shoulder of the person being gifted, and I say, "I gift you with (whatever)."

> You get to decide how simple or elaborate you want your Gifted Ceremony to be.

And then I give the wand to the next person who is doing the gifting.

b. If you are doing the Gifted Ceremony by yourself—and it works to do it by yourself—I would suggest that you choose 13 or less gifts (and write them on strips of paper). Then sit or stand

and open each gift one by one and announce it to yourself, "I gift myself with strength!" Or whatever the gift is. Imagine it soaking into your body, into your cells, into your soul. Do this for each gift. When you're finished, congratulate yourself, and then eat something! Celebrate.

You can give yourself a Gifted Ceremony as many times as you like. They're fun on birthdays or at the beginning of the year. Below are some Gifted Ceremonies, including the one from *Church of the Old Mermaids,* just to refresh your memory, and two others to give you some inspiration.

From *Church of the Old Mermaids:*

One day, Poppy told Sister Laughs a Lot Mermaid that Tulip had nightmares and was afraid to go to sleep at night. Sister Laughs a Lot Mermaid told Grand Mother Yemaya Mermaid and Mother Star Stupendous Mermaid. Grand Mother Yemaya Mermaid said, "Hasn't Tulip been gifted yet?" Poppy told them she had never heard of being Gifted. The Old Mermaids were shocked. "This explains a great deal," said Sister Sophia Mermaid. The others nodded. It did explain a lot.

"In the Old Sea," Mother Star Stupendous Mermaid explained, "every young Old Mermaid has a ceremony, and her mermothers bestow on her various gifts. That's being Gifted."

"That sounds lovely," Poppy said. "Something like that might help Tulip very much."

The Old Mermaids volunteered to be mermothers for Tulip. "And for you," Sister Faye Mermaid said. "Mother and daughter will be Gifted the same!"

Sister Faye Mermaid and Sister Bridget Mermaid organized the ceremony. Sister Ruby Rosarita Mermaid and Sister Lyra Musica Mermaid prepared the feast. Poppy and Sissy Maggie Mermaid made beautiful clothes for Poppy and Tulip—they looked like colorful flashy mermaid tails!

Tulip and Poppy sat out by the pool. When the veil between worlds is supposed to be thinnest, the gifting began. Sister Bridget Mermaid put a seashell necklace around Tulip's neck and Sister Faye Mermaid did the same for Poppy. Then they sang a couple of sea chanties. One by one the Old Mermaids came and stood before Tulip and her mother. Sister DeeDee Lightful Mermaid said, "I gift you with joy!" She kissed the top of Poppy's head, then the top of Tulip's head. Sister Bea Wilder Mermaid came next. "I gift you with ecstatic dance," she said and whirled around. "I gift you with laughter," Sister Laughs A Lot Mermaid said. Then she rubbed her tummy and laughed. She kissed the mother and daughter on the cheek.

> Sister Bridget Mermaid put a seashell necklace around Tulip's neck and Sister Faye Mermaid did the same for Poppy.

"I gift you with enough to eat," Sister Ruby Rosarita Mermaid said. She placed a piece of cake in their laps.

"I gift you with guts!" Sister Sheila Na Giggles Mermaid said. And she shook their hands.

"I gift you with this reminder: you are a part of Nature," Sister Ursula Divine Mermaid said. She gave them each a walking stick made from sycamore branches she had found up on the mountain.

Sister Bridget Mermaid said, "I gift you with poetry and music."

"I gift you with healing and magic," Sister Faye Mermaid said. She turned her closed hands up and opened them. A hummingbird flew off of each palm. I heard tell they glowed, those birds, like lightning bugs. They flew up close to Tulip and Poppy, and then flew away.

I gift you with the mysteries of the Old Sea.

"I gift you with stories," Sister Lyra Musica Mermaid said. She kissed first the mother and then the daughter on the forehead.

"I gift you with wisdom," Sister Sophia Mermaid said.

"I gift you with the stars, the earth, the moon, and the sun," Mother Star Stupendous Mermaid said.

Then Grand Mother Yemaya Mermaid stood before them. Poppy and Tulip got off the chairs and held hands while they awaited Grand Mother Yemaya Mermaid's gift. Grand Mother smiled and said, "I gift you with the mysteries of the Old Sea."

They all cheered and laughed and recited more poetry—then they went and ate the wonderful feast.

Gifted Ceremony at the Old Mermaids Sanctuary for Ana María

The fourteen of them sat in front of a peanut-shaped pool—the Old Mermaids and Ana María. This was not like any human-made pool Ana María had ever seen. In fact, she was not certain how the pool had been created. It was a deep deep blue color. When she glanced at it one way, she could see a mural of a mermaid (one who still had her tails) at the bottom of the pool.

When she looked at it another way, she couldn't see the bottom, only a darkness that seemed to go on indefinitely.

Mother Star Stupendous Mermaid asked Ana María, "Why have you come here?"

"I'm not certain," Ana María said. "I'm in need."

Mother Star Stupendous Mermaid nodded.

"Have you ever been Gifted?" Grand Mother Yemaya Mermaid asked.

The sun was setting when Grand Mother asked this. Ana María looked at the Old Mermaid. For a moment, she thought she could see two beautiful blue-green tails on Grand Mother Yemaya Mermaid. She blinked and she saw only Grand Mother's land legs.

"I've never been gifted at anything in particular," Ana María said.

The Old Mermaids laughed good-naturedly and Ana María smiled.

"Of course you are gifted," Sister Magdelene Mermaid said. "But we are talking about the Gifted ceremony. In the Old Sea, every young Old Mermaid has a Gifted ceremony, and her mermothers bestow on her various gifts. That's being Gifted."

> **In the Old Sea, every young Old Mermaid has a Gifted ceremony, and her mermothers bestow on her various gifts. That's being Gifted.**

"That sounds wonderful," Ana María said. "But I don't think it's for me."

Sister Sophia Mermaid, who asked more questions than any

The Old Mermaids Mystery School **267**

of the other Old Mermaids, immediately wanted to know, "Why isn't it for you?"

"I am not a young Old Mermaid."

"Of course you are!" Sister Lyra Musica Mermaid said. "And even if you weren't, everyone deserves to be gifted. Everyone should know that they are loved and protected as they go through life. Often people forget their gifts so it's good to be reminded."

Grand Mother Yemaya Mermaid said, "We won't push you into anything. This is your home. You are welcome to stay as long as you like."

Ana María nodded. For the first time in a long while, Ana María did feel at home. As though she could grow roots here. As though she could be herself here.

The Old Mermaids showed her a room they had set up just for her. That evening she lay on the bed and tried to sleep but something about the night kept her awake. She went outside to look at the pool. It reflected a million stars. She heard coyotes singing in the distance. Then she heard the sound of wings through the air. When she glanced up, a great-horned owl was flying overhead. The owl landed in the palm tree next to the pool.

> Often people forget their gifts so it's good to be reminded.

Ana María looked at the pool again. The stars shimmered or a breeze rippled the water and she could see the mermaid painted on the bottom of the pool. The mermaid was motioning to her.

Ana María didn't hesitate. She took off all her clothes and then gingerly touched the water with her toes. It was warm.

Ana María jumped into the water. Just like that. She couldn't believe she was doing it. She began swimming. Down below she could see the mermaid in the pool swimming away from her. The mermaid looked back to make certain Ana María was following. Ana María felt free swimming. She felt alive and full of energy. She had not felt this way in a long while.

The mermaid and Ana María swam for a long time. Ana María saw a green light. Something about this green light attracted her. She realized she had been swimming for a long while yet she was not drowning. She looked down at her body and saw that her legs had turned into a tail, a beautiful emerald green tail.

> **She looked down at her body and saw that her legs had turned into a tail, a beautiful emerald green tail.**

When Ana María looked back toward the green light, the mermaid was gone. Ana María kept swimming toward the light. Suddenly, she reached the surface of the water. Her head poked out. She laughed. She had swum back to the pool in the Old Mermaids Sanctuary. It was day now, and all the Old Mermaids stood around the pool.

Sister Ursula Divine Mermaid and Sister Bea Wilder Mermaid both reached down to help her up. Ana María didn't know how she was going to stand after swimming for such a long time—and after growing her tail again!

But she emerged from the water easily. She was a full-grown naked woman; her tail was gone. She looked down at her legs and knew that her tail was not completely gone. It was still a part of her being. Sister Bridget Mermaid and Sister Faye Mermaid wrapped a towel around her.

"I'm ready for my Gifted Ceremony now," Ana María said.

Sister Magdelene Mermaid held out an emerald green gown for her. Ana María stepped into it. Then they led her to a wicker chair with a tall back. The chair was decorated with shells, beads, and flowers. She sat in the chair. One of the Old Mermaids put a cowrie shell necklace over her head and around her neck. The Old Mermaids lined up in front of her: It was an Old Mermaid line, of course, which meant it snaked around the pool.

"Remember, Sister Ana María Mermaid," Grand Mother Yemaya Mermaid said, "that many of these gifts you have had all of your life. Now they will become clearer to you."

> She kissed the top of Ana María's head and Ana María had a glimpse of a mountain lion in her mind's eye.

Sister Sheila Na Giggles Mermaid stepped forward first and said, "I gift you with the ability to see the truth." She touched the middle of Ana María's forehead with her fingers. Then she stepped aside.

"I gift you with the ability to find delight every day," Sister DeeDee Lightful Mermaid said. Sister DeeDee opened her hands and yellow flower petals spilled onto Ana María's lap. Ana María laughed and clapped her hands.

"I gift you with the ability to be full of yourself," Sister Bea Wilder Mermaid said. "With the ability to be full of your true wild self." She kissed the top of Ana María's head and Ana María had a glimpse of a mountain lion in her mind's eye.

Sister Laughs A Lot Mermaid was next. She said, "I gift you with a wicked and wonderful sense of humor and with the ability to laugh."

"I gift you with friends," Sister Lyra Musica Mermaid said, "and the ability to discern who is good for you and who is not."

"I gift you with a love for Nature," Sister Ursula Divine Mermaid said. "With a true connection with Nature."

Sister Bridget Mermaid said, "I gift you with the ability to ask for help."

"I gift you with the ability to be nourished," Sister Ruby Rosarita Mermaid said.

"I gift you with wisdom," Sister Sophia Mermaid said.

Sister Magdelene Mermaid said, "I gift you with love." She kissed both her hands.

"I gift you with the ability to find water and roots wherever you go," Sister Faye Mermaid said. She handed Ana María a mesquite pea pod. "Mesquite trees have the deepest roots of maybe any tree in the world. They are magical and beautiful. They grow in the desert and set their roots deep down into the Earth, as far as 160 feet. They find water wherever it is. They make a home wherever they grow. You can do that, too."

Mother Star Stupendous Mermaid said, "I gift you with the ability to be in the here and now. This is powerful magic."

> Mesquite trees have the deepest roots of maybe any tree in the world. They are magical and beautiful.

Grand Mother Yemaya Mermaid was the last Old Mermaid. Ana María stood up as she approached. Grand Mother took Ana María's hands in her own. The Old Mermaids stood around her.

"I gift you with the knowledge that you are an Old Mermaid and that you always have a place and a home with us. I gift you with the mysteries of the Old Sea."

Grand Mother embraced Ana María. All the Old Mermaids embraced Ana María, and she embraced them. She felt happy. She felt loved. She felt divine! She hardly had the words to describe how she felt.

"Now we celebrate!" Sister Magdelene Mermaid said.

And so they did.

Gifted Ceremony for Jewel

Jewel stepped over the threshold into The Old Mermaids Sanctuary. All the Old Mermaids came out to greet her. Then they took her back to the pool and garden and sat her in a chair.

"It is time for your Gifted Ceremony," Grand Mother Yemaya Mermaid said.

"We are all gifted when we are born," Mother Star Stupendous Mermaid said, "but we often forget, because of life, because of time. Just because. Now we will help you re-member."

The Old Mermaids were dressed in the most beautiful clothes Jewel had ever seen. They seemed to be made from rainbows, bird feathers, wishes, reflections, faery dust, and more or less. Music was playing or coming from the saguaros outside of the garden walls.

> **I gift you with common and uncommon sense.**

Sister Sheila Na Giggles Mermaid came to Jewel first. She kissed the top of her head. "I gift you with common and uncommon sense," she said.

"I gift you with deep wisdom," Sister Sophia Mermaid said as she touched the spot in the middle of Jewel's chest, just below her throat.

Sister Lyra Musica Mermaid said, "I gift you with courage."

"I gift you with constant delight," said Sister DeeDee Lightful Mermaid.

"I gift you with the ability to be wilder," Sister Bea Wilder Mermaid said, "and to bewilder." She laughed. Jewel smiled.

"I gift you with laughter," Sister Laughs A Lot Mermaid said. And she tickled Jewel—who giggled.

Sister Ursula Divine Mermaid growled and gave Jewel a bear hug. "I gift you with presence," she said. "And with the ground beneath your feet."

Sister Bridget Mermaid whistled while she held Jewel's hand. "I gift you with friends."

"I gift you with nourishment," Sister Ruby Rosarita Mermaid said.

> You come from a long line of wise women. And they knew how to root themselves to a place, how to be clear in their own voice.

Sister Magdelene Mermaid kissed Jewel lightly on the lips. "I gift you with love," she said. "With the ability to give it freely and receive it the same."

"I gift you with mystery," Sister Faye Mermaid said.

Grand Mother Yemaya Mermaid and Mother Star Stupendous Mermaid came to Jewel last. They each held one of Jewel's hands and helped her stand.

"We gift you with your lineage," Mother Star Stupendous Mermaid said. "We gift you with the ability to release that which does not serve you. And to hold on to the part of your heritage which will heal and nourish you."

"We gift you with your lineage," Grand Mother Yemaya Mermaid repeated. "You come from a long line of wise women. And they knew how to root themselves to a place, how to be clear in their own voice. How to walk, dance, move through the world and be full of their own true selves. This is your heritage too. We gift you with the ability to embrace and love your true self. This will require practice and commitment, but the way will be easier now because you will know you have been gifted and you've always been gifted."

Jewel didn't know what to say. But then she remembered her throat was open. She remembered she had been given the gift of communication. So she said, "Thank you all."

Practice

1. Create and facilitate a Gifted Ceremony for yourself.
2. Honor the Ancestors.

Journaling

Dreams

Drawing

Mystery Thirteen
Accept Mystery

> Everybody is wondering what and where
> They all came from
> Everybody is worrying about where they're going to go
> When the whole thing's done
> But no one knows for certain and so it's all the same to me
> I think I'll just let the mystery be
> I think I'll just let the mystery be
>
> —Iris de Ment

Here we are at the end of The Old Mermaids Mystery School. These are the mysteries:

Be here now.
Be full of yourself.
Embrace the wild.

Live your siren song.
Cultivate joy.
Be at home in the world.
Encourage your creative process.
Make magic.
Be wise.
Love.
Flow.
Honor the Ancestors.
Accept mystery.

We are at that point when fewer words are needed.

You've experienced the Mysteries. You know that we cannot know everything, we cannot change everything. Sometimes, we need to let the mystery be.

As you finish these Mysteries and carry them with you into the world, I encourage you to accept that you are Nature. You are a part of the ecosystem. You being full of your true self is the greatest gift you can give the world. You are wise, you are loving, you embrace the wild and sing your siren song joyfully, creatively. You do not hide from the world and its challenges. You say, "I am willing," on your terms, to change what needs changing, what is possible to change, to flow with that which is flowing.

You are learning—or have learned—how to connect more deeply with Nature, with the Natural you and with the Nature outside of you. You are learning real magic. It is not like Harry Potter. Magic is about transforming ourselves—and then transforming a condition or situation. Magic is about stepping into flow.

When we are sick or poor or stuck in untenable situations,

we often jump from one thing to another in our desperation to fix that which is broken. It is understandable. Yet sometimes we need to sit with what we have heard, what we have learned, and let it deepen within us. You've heard of Slow Food. The Old Mermaids Mystery School is slow spirituality: a kind of slow connection between ourselves and the world. Give the Mysteries and yourself a chance to Be. And give yourself a pat on the back that you have completed The Old Mermaids Mystery School.

Remember, the stars are singing your praises even as you sing theirs. And that is true of the Entire World. I sing your praises! Thank you so much for being pioneers and true novices in The Old Mermaids Mystery School.

Tale

Sister Faye Mermaid and the Mysteries

Sister Faye Mermaid knew just about everything, except those things she didn't know. And when she didn't know, she relied on her ability to string words together in such a way that time stopped or time sped up or energy flowed or energy swirled and minds were changed and life was transformed. Or it wasn't. Sometimes magic worked. Sometimes it didn't. Or rather, sometimes the answer was yes and sometimes the answer was no. The Universe is a mysterious place.

When Sister Faye Mermaid first arrived on the shores of the New Desert, she was speechless. I don't mean she didn't talk. She wasn't mute. She had no enchantments to sing, no poems to soothe. She knew she had to listen to this new world before she could find the right words. For a while, she did not understand the world. The Old Ems were accustomed to looking to Sister Faye Mermaid when they needed to change the way things were. Yet now, it seemed none of them could change anything.

Wisely, Sister Faye Mermaid began to observe her beloved Old Mermaids as they adjusted to the new world. She noticed how Sister Sheila Na Giggles Mermaid connected herself in the

New Desert through trees. The Old Ems had not had much previous experience with trees, and Sister Faye Mermaid was impressed that Sister Sheila Na Giggles Mermaid figured out the best thing to do for her was to be in this place: be here now.

Sister Faye Mermaid watched as Sister DeeDee Lightful Mermaid struggled at first. She was so accustomed to the milky watery depths. What was she going to do with all the light in the desert? Until she wandered the desert, listened to Coyote Woman, and later found her own light again. She became completely full of herself.

Sister Bea Wilder Mermaid had no idea what to do with herself in the New Desert, but she went out and learned the rhythms of the desert. She completely embraced the wild. Sister Lyra Musica Mermaid conquered her own fears and learned to live her siren song. Although Sister Laughs a Lot Mermaid lost her giggles for a time, she soon began belly laughing as she cultivated joy in the New Desert. And Sister Ursula Divine Mermaid came off the Mountains with a new name—and the ability to be at home in the world.

Sister Bridget Mermaid continued to encourage her own creative process, and Sister Faye Mermaid followed her example as they created songs and enchantments together—even though Sister Faye Mermaid did not feel the magic for a long while.

Sister Ruby Rosarita Mermaid was perhaps the most inspirational of all—even though Sister Faye Mermaid would certainly not rank them! Sister Ruby Rosarita Mermaid learned a new magic: She learned to cook. She transformed ingredients by cutting them up, heating them, cooling them, and/or whispering sweet somethings to them.

Sister Sophia Mermaid never stopped being wise, and she became even wiser, to Sister Faye Mermaid's way of thinking, because she came to understand the New Desert. Likewise, Sister Magdelene Mermaid was always full of love. That never changed.

Grand Mother Yemaya Mermaid was out to sea for a bit when they first arrived in the sandy realms. She soon learned to find her flow in the new world. And Mother Star Stupendous Mermaid continued to stare at the stars, honoring all that had come before them in every step she took.

Sister Faye Mermaid was impressed with her sister Old Mermaids. They had been tossed aside, as it were, tossed ashore in a new world, one they never asked for, one they never longed for, and yet they had all done their best. They had each risen to the occasion, more full of themselves, more knowledgeable, more capable than they had ever been.

> Grand Mother Yemaya Mermaid was out to sea for a bit when they first arrived in the sandy realms. But she soon learned to find her flow in the new world.

As Sister Faye Mermaid walked the desert and contemplated all of this, she realized what was troubling her was that she did not understand what had happened. How had they landed here?

Why? She listened to the coyotes and mockingbirds as she wandered. Listened to the whoosh, whoosh, whoosh as a crow flew overhead in the dry air. She stood in the wash where water sometimes ran, the Sometimes River, and she suddenly realized the reason they had landed here no longer mattered. They were here. They could not go back. She accepted the mystery of it all.

With this realization, her feet settled more deeply into the sand. She felt a breeze tickle the top of her head. And words began to fall from the blue sky, from cacti arms, from the beaks of passing birds. Sister Faye Mermaid felt enchantment all around her in the deep pulsing silence.

The Many Ways of the Old Mermaids

Wisdom lives in everyone,
we suggest you have some fun.

Dance, dance,
be here now.

Fill the world
with your true self.

Find the wild,
it's there inside you.

Sing your song.
Sing it all day long.

Plant the seeds
that bring you joy.

Then make the world
your one true home.

Dive into your creativity:
that is the way of the bountiful sea.

Magic gets made
by folks like you,

So use your wisdom
in all you do.

Offer love to one and all;
It's the best way for all to glow.

Then open up your beautiful heart
to the joyful endless universal flow.

Honor all the beings
that came before you,

And hold the mystery
in all you do.

These hints for living
are our true gifts

to raise your spirits.
They're mermaid lifts!

—Mario Milosevic

Practice

A Gifted Ceremony for Someone Else

You have all been on a kind of pilgrimage during these 13 mysteries. As is true for all good pilgrimages, it's time to bring what you've learned home. You created a Gifted Ceremony for yourself. Now you will create a Gifted Ceremony for someone else. It can be a friend, spouse, child. Mario and I have created a Gifted Ceremony twice for our neighbor, once when she was 10 and once when she was 11, and she loved it. She asked for the second one. Of course, she grew up with the Old Ems and she loves mermaids, so she was a natural.

I imagine that you've already got someone in mind. You can ask them if they want a Gifted Ceremony, explain to them what it is, and go from there. Once you have the person you are going to "gift," then plan the ceremony. First take a journey to your Old Mermaids Sanctuary, and ask the Old Mermaids for 13 gifts, just as you did for yourself. Or come up with gifts yourself. Remember that the gifts should be general and not too specific. Make certain none of the gifts reflect any underlying agendas.

For instance if you're gifting your neighbor who is in a bad marriage, don't gift her with a "divorce." You can always gift her with "love" instead. Or if you are gifting your daughter, and you want her to go to college and she doesn't want to go, don't gift her with a "college degree." In this case, don't even gift her with knowledge or education. Steer clear of it. The Gifted Ceremony should never have any strings attached.

You've done a Gifted Ceremony for yourself. You know what you liked and didn't like. You can use your Gifted Ceremony as a template to create one for someone else. As you do it, remember to be full of yourself. You have embodied your true self, and you are spreading the gifts of the Old Mermaids out into the world. Have fun and enjoy yourself.

Practice

1. Create and facilitate a Gifted Ceremony for someone else.

2. Congratulate yourself on completing The Old Mermaids Mystery School!

3. That's it! You did it! Finis!

The Rest is Mystery.

About the Author

Kim Antieau's books include many accounts of the Old Mermaids and their adventures in the Old Sea and the New Desert. Among them are *Church of the Old Mermaids, The Fish Wife,* and *The Blue Tail.* She has also distilled much of the wisdom of the Old Mermaids into several non-fiction books, including *The Old Mermaids Book of Days and Nights* and *The Old Mermaid's Oracle.* Her other books include *The Jigsaw Woman, Whackadoodle Times, Ruby's Imagine, Queendom: Feast of the Saints, Monster's Daughter, Killing Beauty, Coyote Cowgirl, Under the Tucson Moon, The Salmon Mysteries,* and *Answering the Creative Call.* She lives in the Southwest with her husband, Mario Milosevic.

Learn more about Kim's writing at her website: kimantieau.com. Find Kim's photographs at kimantieau.smugmug.com. Get exclusive access to new content and support Kim and Mario's creative projects at www.patreon.com/kimandmario.

The Thirteen Suggestions

Get the starfish outta your eyes, sister.
Sister Sheila Na Giggles Mermaid

Step lightly. Dance hard. Eat your vegetables.
Sister DeeDee Lightful Mermaid

Things change. Get over it.
Sister Bea Wilder Mermaid

Fear has no sisters, but I have many.
Sister Lyra Musica Mermaid

She who laughs a lot laughs a lot.
Sister Laughs A Lot Mermaid

I am most at home where the wild things are.
Sister Ursula Divine Mermaid

Sing, dance, create. If you have to choose one,
do all three at once.
Sister Bridget Mermaid

A good bean is hard to find. Everything else is easy.
Sister Ruby Rosarita Mermaid

Go with the flow—and watch out for waterfalls.
Sister Sophia Mermaid

You ask me to tell you about love? Showing is so much better.
Sister Magdelene Mermaid

Laugh or weep. We swim in your tears.
Grand Mother Yemaya Mermaid

All the wisdom of the ages can be distilled
into one suggestion: Be.
Mother Star Stupendous Mermaid

The rest is . . . mystery.
Sister Faye Mermaid

The Thirteen Mysteries

Be Here Now
Be Full of Yourself
Embrace the Wild
Live Your Siren Song
Cultivate Joy
Be at Home in the World
Encourage Your Creative Process
Make Magic
Be Wise
Love
Flow
Honor the Ancestors
Accept the Mystery

www.ingramcontent.com/pod-product-compliance
Lightning Source LLC
Chambersburg PA
CBHW081740100526
44592CB00015B/2245